PAINTING
and
LINING
In the smaller scales

BY
STEVE BARNFIELD

FOR
DENISE,
WHO UNDERSTANDS.

Copywrite Irwell Press 1994
ISBN 871608-55-4

First Published in the United Kingdom
by
IRWELL PRESS,
15 Lovers Lane,
Grasscroft,
Oldham, OL4 4DP

Printed by The Amadeus Press, Huddersfield

CONTENTS

INTRODUCTION AND ACKNOWLEDGEMENTS

'Lord Howe' from the limited edition **CRAFTSMAN MODELS** kit. Nothing special - just a straight forward painting and lining job with Precision Paints Malachite Green. This is the sort of bread and butter jobs I like - a good kit to put together followed by a nice user friendly paint job.

Writing this book has, I have to say, not been the easiest thing I've ever done. Some readers may consider that there are elements of teaching Grandmother To Suck Eggs, but bear with me, as not everybody has the same amount of experience. So, if you find a chapter or two rather run of the mill stuff or not to your taste perhaps because you feel that you have already been there and done it, please remember those who haven't. Knowing what to put in and what to leave out is always a problem, so I've erred on the side of thoroughness.

I am assuming that the modellers who read this little book (having, hopefully, purchased it!) will have a wide variation in skill and approach to painting models. I must, therefore, beg the reader's indulgence, and apologise if some favourite method or technique is not included. After all, there is always more than one way to get from A to B and still arrive at a desired result. This is so very true of modelling; not all of us use the same methods, but that doesn't matter as long as we get there in the end, and achieve what we have set out to do. This is the purpose of this book - to help the reader arrive, and perhaps shorten the journey a little bit! In addition, I must point out that this book, aimed as it is at the beginner as well as the more experienced modeller who wishes to improve his techniques, will mostly cover 4mm and 7mm scales. However,

the methods outlined can be, and I'm sure are, employed in other scales. I will concentrate mostly on materials and equipment that are readily available from model shops and town centre stockists, or from traders at exhibitions. A few of the materials I use, though, are only obtainable from more specialist retailers, and are sometimes difficult to find. I have found though, that there is often an alternative, and most shops will be helpful in sorting out something which will suit.

A Bit of Background

My own modelling interests and skills have been developed over many years, at first as a hobby. That started when my parents bought me (inevitably) a Tri-ang train set for Christmas in 1955 - not that I could get near it, as father and various assorted uncles had to have a go first! I wish I still had it - it must be quite a collector's item by now. I suppose I then went through the possibilities that most boys (and some girls) of my generation tried - plastic model aeroplanes, the extended train set, Meccano and so on. I was never an inveterate train spotter, however, something which I now regret. Those, of course, were the days of the two shilling (proper money) Airfix kits, which all needed to be painted. One a week from Woolworth's on a Saturday morning was my norm, until other things (which somehow seemed more important at the time) took over.

We complain bitterly about the standard of instructions in kits today, but those in Airfix kits were excellent, and apart from getting the cement (no Mek-Pak in those days) all over the place, they were dead easy to put together. Then came the painting. In the more expensive kits - the ones costing about five bob, a fortune in those days - Airfix paint was supplied in little squeezy capsules. For the rest, as far as I can remember there were two sorts of tinlets available: the ubiquitous Humbrol and the Airfix 'own brand'. Back in those days, the range of colours was nowhere near that available now, while (I remember) it was soon apparent that full gloss finish on small scale models was NOT RIGHT. Then, one day, I watched a cousin painting a lorry and *she* painted the tyres *matt black*. This was a revelation, and from then on I thought more about finish and how this is perceived by different people.

In perhaps twenty years of professional model making, I have always had a tendency to get used to and stick to methods which, although perfectly adequate for me and what I do, perhaps don't suit everyone. However, what I can say is that as they do work for me, there's every chance that they will work for others. I am a great believer in keeping things as simple as possible, and can see no point in over-complicating things when it is not necessary. If you have a system which

3

works, whether it be painting and lining or to do with any other part of the hobby, stick to it, and only change if the benefits obtained really make it worth while. Wouldn't life be boring if everyone did everything the same! Obviously, I have not been able to try everything on the market which is suitable for the hobby but of those products I have tried (as you will see from later chapters in the book), several have suited my own methods and tastes. What this means is, although I can recommend the materials and methods I use, there may be others.

I will gloss (!) over some of the more expensive items of painting equipment, such as spray guns for use with cellulose, as I think these fall outside the scope of these pages. Although cellulose paint is readily available, it is not the easiest of materials to work with. With the exception of those ubiquitous spray cans, cellulose needs a different approach to that traditional modelling medium, enamel paint. Where I mention it, this is only for completeness.

Rather than mix up in the text the names and addresses of various suppliers used or recommended, these appear at the end of the book in the *Sources Index.*

The Skidmore Legacy

I have to confess that I really took up painting and lining my own models, and those I built to commission, because of the cost of having somebody else do the work. This may seem somewhat hypocritical, but I feel relatively lucky that having picked a few brains and had a go, I found that with practice I soon developed the necessary skills. Such methods, which nowadays earn me a modest crust, aren't necessarily my own copyright. In acknowledging those who put me on the right road, as it were, one name immediately springs to mind - that of Mike Skidmore. Many people will remember Mike as part of the team at the long-lamented Millholme Models, the shop that seemed to stock everything. Now under new ownership as a producer of white metal kits only, Millholme Models was, in the 1970s, as well known as any model shop at the time. Mike was the resident guru on all matters concerned with painting and lining, and was always very free with friendly advice and encouragement. It was he who put me on to Floquil paint, the importance of a good bowpen and the many advantages of a good airbrush.

When Mike had to give up model painting through ill health some years ago he kindly donated to me some of his equipment, which I still use. It is because of the help and inspiration that I have had from people like Mike that I like to do the odd demonstration or talk at exhibitions, and hence pass on some of the hints and tips which I have been given, together with those I've developed over the years.

Another guiding light was John Fowler, who opened his Peterborough Model Shop at about the time I was becoming seriously interested in model railways. John gave me my first commission, and I still remember my fight with that BSL Gresley! It was also John who sold me one of the original Trix 'Flying Scotsman' models, and on querying the boiler band lining he it was who introduced me to the old Kings Cross 'Kingsprint' rub down transfers - setting me on the loco-painting road.

John was not everybody's cup of tea, and did not suffer fools gladly, but he built up a thriving business, still one of the best model railway specialist shops that I know of. John was a terrific help and encouragement to me, and to many other modellers in the area. His son, Chris, now runs the shop, and very helpful he is too, but he will I'm sure be the first to admit that he's different from his dad.

I must also thank my customers over the years for plying me with their trade. It is always very pleasing to produce a model to the customer's satisfaction, and I must say this still gives me a considerable buzz.

**Steve Barnfield,
Peterborough, 1994**

Passing on a tip or two. Demonstrating at the Blairgowerie Modellers' weekend.

Chapter One

PREAMBLE

Livery Colours

There is much discussion in the hobby about whether or not this or that colour is 'correct'. Modellers who say that they can remember colours from their own childhood do themselves no favours - it is hardly possible to carry a particular shade of colour in the memory for longer than a few seconds, never mind fifty years! What *is* possible, though, is to judge whether a shade looks right to *you*. However, as individuals, we all perceive colour differently, and until a time machine is invented the arguments will rage on. I sometimes feel that there is far too much time spent in debating whether this or that colour is right; there are as many opinions on this subject as there are colours, and if you the modeller have chosen a colour to suit you and you think it is right, then so be it!

Think about this. Some years ago, I was in conversation with an elderly gent at a talk I had given on painting and lining; he told me that as a boy before the war he had been an apprentice at Doncaster works. While going about his work one afternoon, he saw two ex-works Gresley Pacifics in the paint shop yard - and noticed they were not the same shade of green. There was not much in it, but the difference was distinct. Upon enquiry, it turned out that one had been painted on the day shift, the other on

the night shift. Two paintshop foremen, who presumably mixed the paint to the same recipe, had arrived at slightly differing results. No nipping down to the local DIY for a couple of cans of Dulux here - paints were actually mixed on site immediately before use, using raw pigments and linseed oil.

After I had heard this account, and I see no reason to disbelieve the gentleman, I gave up worrying whether the particular shade of LNER green I was using was an absolute 'dead ringer', and resolved to please myself. If I and those I painted for were happy, then that was what mattered. What is true of LNER green is equally true of other colours; look at the argument that has gone on for years about 'Midland Red'. This is the colour also known as 'Crimson Lake', and according to the latest research, the constituents going to make up this shade did not change over the years from when the Midland Railway introduced it in the later part of the nineteenth century until 1948, when the LMS was calling it 'Maroon'. The shade re-introduced by BR in the mid-1950s was also apparently identical in composition.

Bob Forster, who has done a great deal of research into paint and how it was applied to the prototype, tells me that the shade of Crimson Lake ordered from the manufacturer by the

LMS was always matched to a 1913 Midland Railway sample. The perceived difference of shade which resulted derived from the way in which this paint was applied, not in the actual paint itself. It is well known that the Midland were very keen on finish of the highest quality, but that the LMS, although still desiring a lasting result did cheapen the process by cutting down the number of top coats and varnishes. Later in the book, when we actually get down to particular examples, I quote the British Railways specification for coach painting, where it is interesting to note that the maroon colour is in fact specified as 'Crimson'!

The Effects of Lining

The arguments still go on though, with some people claiming that the shade of Midland Red became lighter over the years. It is probable that this conception has arisen through another factor which influences the perception of colour - colour area. A couple of changes may have given rise to this factor coming into the picture; firstly, the Midland changed the way their locomotives were lined, from particularly complicated to fairly simple, and secondly, the locomotives to which the livery was applied became larger. These changes meant larger areas of the background colour were not broken up by lining. The more lining there is on a locomotive, the darker the background colour will look, for not only is the lining influencing the eyes' perception of the base colour, but it is also breaking up the background into smaller areas. And a small area of paint will always appear darker than a large expanse of the same colour.

Weathering of Paint

Until the 1950s paint technology remained fairly basic, although some ingredients did change. Paint manufacturers mixed batches of paints to match a master 'colour card', which would have been in use for a number of years. The pigments which went to make up the same colour over, say, fifty years might be radically different, but the result would have been the same. However, what *did* vary was the way the colour reacted once it was applied. The different ingredients would not all 'weather' the same way in use. Atmospheric conditions also changed with time, and the pigments used to mix the paint could react in differing ways, some, for instance, fading more than others. Blues were notorious for this, and fading was one of the reasons why it was abandoned for express locos by British Railways in the early 1950s.

Varnishes also changed as paint formulation was improved over the years. At one time the varnishes applied to locos and rolling stock were nowhere near as transparent as they are today, those in the nineteenth century being particularly dark. As varnish lightened and became clearer with time, so the true colour of the paint beneath showed through. Here is an-

other explanation for the perceived shade of 'Midland Crimson' lightening over the years, although as we've now established the paint was never changed.

Another example of varnish altering the perceived colour is that of GWR Cream. Originally, it was specified in 1864 by the directors of the company as follows all coaches should be painted *white* [my emphasis] above the waistline. However, white was not the colour observed from the lineside, and it is almost certain that it was the varnish which imparted to the white the appearance of pale cream. In 1880, the official colour *was* changed to 'cream', but the continued use of a darker varnish resulted in the shade yellowing markedly. Research has shown that no official change took place after then, but as the paint ingredients and technology changed, so did the apparent shade of the paint, back to a pale cream by 1935. Today, with modern technology, railway paints are produced under computer control and are rarely varnished, so one tin box on wheels looks pretty much the same shade as the next one along.

Atmospheric Influences

Different atmospheric conditions would affect paint in varying ways. Imagine the prevailing conditions in, say, Leeds and Penzance; there couldn't be two places that would have differed more. No disrespect to Leeds, but I know where I would like to live when considering what the atmosphere must have been like up to the 1960s! We hear much talk about acid rain now, but the pollution during the

age of steam was infinitely worse. The chemical reactions of these pollutants with the various mixtures of paint pigments and varnishes would have been different depending on location and even the type of coal used. The effect of all this, allied to the inevitable accretions of dirt, was kept at bay by an army of cleaners who used various methods to try and stay the worst. However, these activities would also affect the surface and locos or coaches, even if painted at the same time, would soon start to differ remarkably depending upon location, type of traffic worked, and local cleaning techniques.

The Uncertain Conclusion

For all these reasons, we cannot be too pedantic about whether this shade or that shade of paint is correct. The effect of these varying atmospheric conditions would make some colours fade, while others would deepen, until no two locos would look the same. I am always highly suspicious when I'm told that this or that particular colour *must* be right because it has been matched to a sixty year old paint chip taken from a locomotive when it was scrapped. How do we know what had affected that sample of paint before it was taken from the prototype? If it had been matched to a manufacturers sample painted at the same time as the locomotive, which had been sealed up away from any outside influences, it may be that this could be taken as representing the 'correct' colour. However, even in that event, it could be that aging of the paint would alter the chemical composition, and hence col-

Midland Railway 'M' Class c.1900. In some respects, at this time, the Midland livery was amongst the most flambouyant of all. In 4mm scale this type of livery can be difficult to render convincingly, so it is important to get as fine a line as possible.

MR 700 Class still in Crimson Lake livery but in the simplfied form introduced by Deeley. The two photos demonstrate the importance of getting your research correct, and as can be seen here there is much less lining. A single yellow line has been painted on the front boiler band and another at the rear of the firebox. Etched boiler bands come out far too thick!

our, as the materials used then were not as stable as those used now. If the reader concludes that I am very sceptical about 'accurate colour', he would be right.

If we are modelling all the rolling stock on the layout as though it had - quite improbably - come straight out of the works, then there may be some relevance in academically correct col-

ours. If, however, we are going to try for a certain amount of realism on the model railway, then a certain amount of 'weathering' is more or less a must. I have to say that until a few years ago I wasn't really sure of this, but if done properly, there is no doubt that such a finish does look extremely convincing.

The Case for Spraying

As with any job, certain equipment is necessary to carry out particular tasks, and the painting and lining of models is no different in this respect. As always, some tools are essential while others, although helpful, may be more of a luxury. Therefore, before we get on to doing anything specific, it is necessary to decide what basic equip-

The importance of having a good photograph or photographs has been stressed many times by others. I concurr - it is also important to have a clear photo or two showing livery details as far as can be seen. Here No.108 (ex.4477) GAY CRUSADER is turned out in post -War LNER Green, but is no different from its pre-War version. Note that the lettering lines up with the numbers on the cab side and not the middle of the lining panel.

ment we need. Which, in turn, means we need to decide on our basic painting technique - brush or spray?

A finish that has been sprayed on to your model will, in my experience, be far superior to any obtained with an ordinary paint brush. I have to say, therefore, that spraying is, in my opinion, an absolute necessity - although that doesn't mean you have to use an airbrush. I have seen excellent results obtained with spray cans whether they are of the kind supplied by specialist paint-makers such as Humbrol, or automotive cellulose types from the local motor accessory shop. So, first of all, I am assuming that the modeller will want to acquire, has already pur-

chased, or have access to, some sort of spraying equipment. This is not to say that ordinary paintbrushes do not have their place; they do, particularly for painting smaller items or sub-assemblies, so I won't ignore them. Airbrushes, however, are such excellent tools to have and handle that once you have used one and got the hang of it you will wonder how you ever managed without it.

There are not now many modellers of note who continue to brush paint their models, but there are a few diehards. One convert who was for a long time very averse to using an airbrush is Mike Sharman. Mike is always willing to show me his latest creation (he

scratch builds early Victorian locomotives, mostly in 4mm scale) and I have to admit that some of the results he obtained with an ordinary paintbrush were very close to being as good as an airbrush finish. This is perhaps why it took me a long time to persuade him to have a go with the airbrush, but once he tried one he was soon converted, and now he uses it for virtually all his paintwork.

Of course, the airbrush can't stand alone; there has to be some way of actually getting paint on to the model. Although we will be looking in greater detail at all the options, it is important not to overlook the effects of propellant used, whether this is in conjunction with an airbrush or simply in the context of a spray can. As well as the varying effectiveness of the different types of propellant systems in getting the paint onto the model, there are HEALTH IMPLICATIONS in the use of some canned gases.

Spray Painting Safety

If we are going to spray paint onto a model, then a spraying booth of some sort ought to be considered vital. At the most basic, a large cardboard box used out in the garden will suffice to contain overspray and perhaps prevent dust from settling on the model as it dries. However, these are only two of the considerations affecting the use of paint in spray form. Many model paints contain quite potent and volatile organic solvents, such as benzene, toluene and xylene, and these have a number of hazards associated with them. Such solvents are toxic by inhalation or by swallowing, are skin irritants and can have carcinogenic effects. They are also highly inflammable. For these reasons, it is important to ensure that we don't expose ourselves to health risks when spraying some types of paints.

Obviously, good ventilation is vital, but if the job is going to be done properly then a spray booth with a suitable extractor fan and a vent to the outside atmosphere should be considered. This will remove overspray, fumes and smell, as well as most of the atomised paint and thinners. My own booth is home made to suit me, and is shown in the photographs. Although it has served me well with no problems for a number of years, it is perhaps a little crude by current standards.

Recommendations nowadays are for the use of an indirect system of extraction with a fibrous filter between the spray chamber and the fan. To be absolutely safe, the fan itself should also be of the flameproof type, using a brushless motor. Alternatively, it can be belt driven from a remotely mounted motor, so that volatile paint fumes don't come into direct contact with the motor. A booth of this type, designed for the magazine 'Modelling Railways Illustrated', is also shown in the diagrams. An extractor (ie, vent to outside wall) cooker hood, which incor-

A Mike Sharman model - 'Mac's Mangle' was an early LNWR engine with apredilection for demolishing platform edges. Mike painted this using my airbrush techniques.

porates a filter and is designed to do much the same sort of job, could also be pressed into service and built into a simple cabinet. It may not, however, have enough throughput to do a 100% job on paint fumes, especially where larger models are being sprayed.

To protect your respiratory system from the ingesting of harmful vapours and paint particles, it is also a very good idea to wear some sort of mask. The only truly effective ones are those incorporating an activated charcoal filter cartridge, ideally with a paint droplet pre-filter. Most motor industry paint suppliers and the better DIY outlets will stock these. More details are in the sources index. However, as with all things, these precautions are a matter of degree; if you're only spraying the odd small model occasionally, then you're not likely to come to much harm if you work in well ventilated conditions and avoid as far as possible inhaling paint fumes. But if you're doing a lot of paint jobs and working indoors, then you do need to heed the cautions.

If you think that all this gloom and doom and talk of risks seems a bit excessive, this may be because it is only relatively recently that the full health implications of spraying synthetic enamel type paints with a toluene or xylene-based thinner and carrier medium have been realised. These nasties are currently present in a lot of model paints, including aerosols, but the paint industry is rapidly moving away from such formulations in favour of water-based acrylic polymers, which are far more environmentally-friendly and have very low health risks. In the USA, my old favourite, Floquil, which is xylene-based, and is starting to be replaced by Badger 'Accu-Flex' and Floquil's own 'Poly S', both water-based acrylics, while in this country Humbrol's 'Hobby Acrylic' is also beginning to become popular in the general model paint world. The ever-changing paint technology already discussed is still moving forward, even in the hobby field.

My spray booth - in need of a clean! Actually, it looks a lot worse then it is. This pair of Kirk, Gresley wooden coach sides have just received a coat of varnish - fundamental to the whole process of spaying, of course, is your safety. Its important to have good lighting, plenty of room and a large extractor fan.

The alternative Rice booth.

Chapter Two

PREPARING FOR THE PAINT

Clean and ready to go.

It should go without saying that before any paint is applied to a model it should be free from anything which will stop the paint from sticking to it. In some respects this is the most important part of painting a model, as anything which comes afterwards cannot disguise the fact that the model wasn't cleaned adequately. It is also no good blaming the paint for not sticking if the surface beneath was not prepared properly in the first place. However, before worrying about cleaning the surface for painting, there are a couple of other considerations to take into account.

Sub-Assemblies

When building a model locomotive myself, I try and arrange the construction so as to split the model into as many sub-assemblies as possible. Keeping the chassis separate from the body is obvious, as are separate bogie and pony trucks where applicable. However, it is usually possible without too much trouble to arrange for the main parts of the locomotive body itself to fit together using one or two small screws instead of solder or glue. I wonder sometimes about the thought processes of many loco kit designers, particularly at the lower end of the market, who apparently give no con-

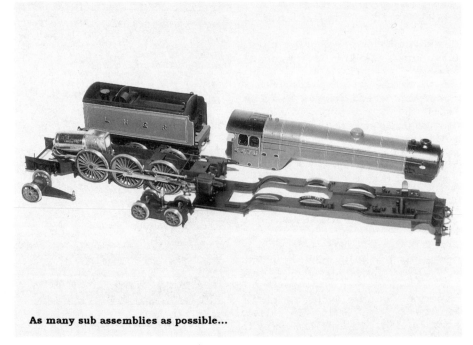

As many sub assemblies as possible...

sideration at all to the painting of a model, and advise in the instructions to glue or solder everything up as one unit, sometimes so that not even the bogies and pony trucks can be removed. To the inexperienced modeller, this can make painting very difficult, especially as he/she won't have the practical know-how to arrange things any better.

When assembling kits, it is well worth planning ahead as you build, to see whether a sub-assembly or two can be left for attachment after painting. As you can see from the photographs, with a little thought it can usually be done. Even those kits that just aren't designed this way can sometimes, with a certain amount of thought and pre-planning, be re-engi-

A well designed NER Class 290 white metal kit by Owen Lancaster. The rear of the firebox slides nicely into the cab front and the boiler assembly is held in place with one screw under the smokebox.

L&Y Barton Wright 0-6-0. The finished article, below, is finished in black but is fully lined. Again the boiler assembly is held in place by a couple of screws under the smokebox.

A step up again for surface preparation, come the small shotblasting cabinets, which in your author's opinion really are the bees knees. They use a similar material to that used in the Badger gun, and in some respects are a much bigger and far more sophisticated version of the same thing. I am very lucky in having access to one, which I tend to use more on models in the larger scales. The big, big, snag, however, for the average hobbyist is the cost - getting on for four figures when all the necessary ancillary equipment, such as compressor, air tank and extractor fan has been taken into account.

Surface Filling

During the construction phase I also take the opportunity of filling any small blow holes in castings with either low melt solder or cellulose filler. If using the latter, I prefer the two part stuff as it becomes hard quite quickly, and can be worked after only a short time. There are several varieties of these resin-based fillers available, and I generally use Davids 'Isopon P38'. There are others, such as 'Plastic Padding' and Holts 'Cataloy', that seem to be similar. Most DIY stores, as well as branches of Halfords and other car accessory shops, stock this type of product, as may the local garage. The trick in using these fillers is to apply them with a pliable spatula. I normally use a small piece of plastic card for this and work the resin paste well in to the surface. I sometimes wonder about modellers who don't bother to do this, as it seems to me a very basic

neered to give manageable sub-assemblies. If you can do it, it's well worth the effort.

Preparing the Surface

Over the years, I have developed my own methods for ensuring that the the surface of my models is in the right state to receive paint. Basically, the model needs to be totally clean - not just free from grease and dirt, but also from any blobs of glue or solder left behind from construction. All such contamination needs to be removed before any painting can be started. A method I have adopted is to regularly clean the model as it is being built with a fibre glass pencil and a small brass suede brush. This also highlights any imperfections in the surface of the model, and the resulting fine surface abrasion will also help the paint to stick.

A rather more sophisticated version of this method of preparing the surface is the Badger Abrasive Gun. This uses the same propulsion systems as an airbrush and scours the surface of the model with fine aluminium oxide powder, leaving it in an ideal condition to receive paint. The model should be washed both before and after using the gun. The gun is rather wasteful of

Rubbing over the surface with a fibre - glass brush

the powder, and therefore should be used in such a way that as much of the powder as possible can be collected and recycled. Ideally, an enclosed cabinet should be used. If not, care should be taken to avoid getting the powder into your lungs - a dust mask is essential. Don't let it anywhere near the compressor either, as being abrasive it will do the bearings no good at all...

job; models so treated will look much better for very little extra effort.

Cleaning and De-greasing

As a start, it is a good idea not to let the model get too dirty in the first place, and regular cleaning during construction can help prevent this. I normally wash with a liquid cleanser (see below) every evening, or after each

The occasional dig or scratch is inevitable - but never fear; fill with two parts resin and rub smooth with wet and dry - lovely finish.

building session. This obviously stops a build up of flux, swarf and grease, as well as giving me a chance to examine my work carefully under the best conditions. The real trouble in cleaning often comes with a model I receive for painting ready built, where I sometimes need to adopt a different and more drastic approach, particularly with the chassis.

There are a number of options available to clean and de-grease a model, and my preferred method is to wash thoroughly, first with a washing up liquid and then with a liquid cream cleanser. The washing up liquid is good at removing grease, while the liquid cleanser removes dirt and the residual lanolin from the washing up liquid. That's what is put in to keep your hands as soft as your face, but it's no help in encouraging paint to stick. I suppose this double dose seems a bit of a belt and braces job, but it is better, to use an old cliche, to be safe rather than sorry. The best tools for this washing are an old soft toothbrush or (I have found) a one inch paint brush.

A good lather can be worked up using either brush or cleaning agent, followed by a thorough rinse after each application. The final rinse is, of course, the most important, as every scrap of the cleanser must be washed away. Sometimes, if sufficient quantities of clean water aren't used for rinsing, small white specks are left behind. These can appear as little specks in

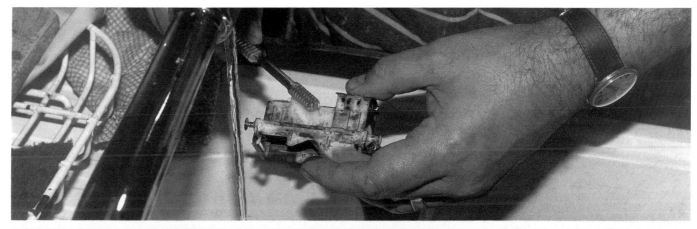

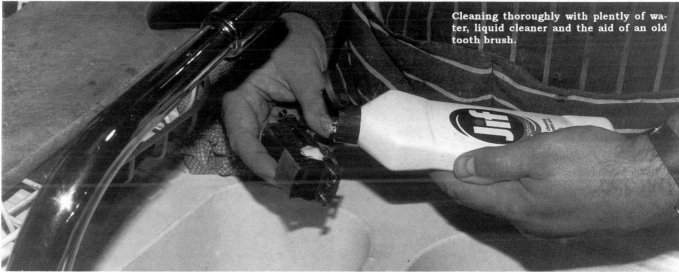

Cleaning thoroughly with plenty of water, liquid cleaner and the aid of an old tooth brush.

the paint.

Some modellers don't like this method, as there is a chance that scrubbing will detach small items. While you do need to give the model a thorough clean, there is no need to scrub violently. If items do fall off during cleaning, then they were not fixed properly in the first place. The chances are they will become loose after the model has been painted and finished, with disastrous results; it is much easier to re-fix details to an unpainted model. It is, however, sensible to scrub and rinse over a container to catch anything that *should* happen to fall off.

Chassis Cleaning

With a running chassis, it is normally either impossible or imprudent to remove the wheels and coupling rods without affecting the running qualities. In these cases, the chassis needs to be cleaned and de-greased in a different way, and the most reliable method I have found (without recourse to expensive ultrasonic baths) is to use a solvent, such as xylene. As already noted in the spraying precautions, such volatile chemicals should be used with the utmost care in well ventilated conditions, preferably using the filter mask to prevent inhalation of the fumes. Slater's Mek-Pak, sold as liquid plastic cement, is also good, and is of course more readily available from model shops. However, if there are any plastic parts on the model, steer clear

of the powerful solvents like xylene or Mek, as these will attack most modelling plastics.

Slater's also sell a 'Track and Mechanism Cleaner' which is a milder and plastic-compatible cleaner/degreaser, whilst similar de-greasing 'switch cleaners' can be bought in aerosol cans from electronics suppliers such as Tandy. Make sure that you get a non-lubricating variety, however, as some contain silicones which are good for oiling switch mechanisms but useless under paint. An alternative to all these

solvents is an etching cleaner such as Carr's Acid Dip. I have to say, though, that I don't find these nearly as effective.

An old small paintbrush can be used to get into all the nooks and crannies of the chassis, particularly behind the wheels and anywhere oil is likely to accumulate or penetrate. It may sometimes be necessary to repeat the application of cleaner two or three times to remove all the grease and debris. Of course, there is no reason why the rest of the model can't have the same

Handling the clean model using surgical gloves.

treatment, but I would still advise a wash as already described.

Drying

Once satisfied that the model is as clean as it will get, it needs to be dried thoroughly. I have two usual methods here. If in a hurry, I use a hair dryer, but if you're not careful this can result in parts coming adrift, particularly if they've been attached with low melt solder. It is surprising just how much heat a small hairdryer will generate. Perhaps my second approach is the best way, leaving the model in a well ventilated box in the airing cupboard or some other such warm, dry place overnight. The box needs to be well ventilated to allow the water vapour to escape as the model dries. An inverted shoebox with holes made in the sides and ends with an office punch is effective.

Handling the Clean Model

With the model clean and degreased, it is important that it is not handled with greasy or sticky fingers. Of course, the sensible modeller will have thought of this, and provided himself with some means of handling the model without touching the prepared surfaces. A wire through a buffer socket, perhaps, to suspend the model? Or a block of wood jammed in the motor cut-out of a boiler, or maybe a small hand vice clamped to some unseen internal part. It is usually possible to find some way of making a 'handle'.

Although I find that well washed hands will not affect the cleaned surface if you are quick, such handling is not really recommended. Wear the dis-

posable surgical gloves now widely available very cheaply from the local chemist. These are also a good idea when handling or mixing paint and thinners; for reasons already noted, you want to avoid getting those materials on your hands.

Stripping

Before going on to the next chapter, where paint will actually get on to the

surface of the model, a word or two about stripping. Not the sort which makes some people's eyes light up, but removing paint from a model when it is no longer needed. Once, many years ago, John Fowler of the Peterborough model shop asked me to repaint a loco for him - a Wills J39 as I recall. Nothing too remarkable in that I don't suppose there were more than a dozen parts to the kit at that date, but I made

'Modelstrip' about to be applied to the factory finish of this Alco RS11 switcher plastic body shell.

the big mistake of dunking the whole thing in Nitromors paint stripper. What nobody had told me was that strong paint strippers actually dissolve epoxy resin adhesives like Araldite, and so a simple repaint turned in to a complete rebuild. I pass this on in the hope that others may not be as silly as me, although on the plus side this is a good way of retrieving a hopelessly badly-built and painted whitemetal kit, something that can often be bought very cheaply.

I still use Nitromors for paint stripping, but no longer dunk the whole model in it. It is quite a powerful and caustic mixture of chemicals, so a lot of care is needed in handling it. What I do now is to coat half the surface of the model with stripper, using the ubiquitous soft toothbrush and a stippling action, leave for a minute or two, then lightly scrub to remove the softened paint. Depending on how well the paint has been put on, a second or third application of Nitromors is sometimes needed. The model can then be rinsed off under the cold tap, using washing up liquid to help remove the softened paint. It is also worth remembering that although virtually any paint can be applied on top of cellulose, the reverse is not true. Cellulose will attack enamel paint, for instance, so if you make a mess of putting enamel on to a model, a wash with cellulose thinners will remove it.

Stripping paint from plastic bodies can be a real pain, as ordinary strippers will promptly dissolve the plastic as quickly as the paint. In the past, brake fluid has proved effective at fetching off paint, but over the years seems it seems to have lost its bite. However, products such as 'Modelstrip' are specially formulated for stripping paint from plastic. Available in pots from model shops, 'Modelstrip' is a paste that is applied in a thick layer over the model, which is then sealed in a polythene bag and left overnight. In the morning, the paint can be simply washed off under a running tap, scrubbing the model gently with an old soft toothbrush. Sometimes, depending on the age of the paint and also how many coats there are, a number of applications may be necessary. There are one or two factory finishes, such as some of Hornby's, that neither 'Modelstrip' nor brake fluid will touch. These are a problem, and may have to be overpainted, never a good idea if you can avoid it.

From the top: 1.Brushing on the 'Modelstrip' (rubber gloves an important precaution); 2. make sure you cover the entire surface with about a 2mm thick layer; 3. cook in the bag overnight; 4. plenty of water and an old tooth brush help remove the clag; 5.an undamaged, unpainted body ready for the off.

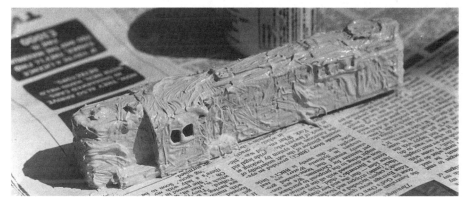

Chapter Three

PRIMING AND UNDERCOATING

Why Prime?

The importance of the priming stage in obtaining a good paint finish on models is often overlooked. Apart from its primary function - helping the livery colours to adhere properly to the surface of metal models - a coat of primer is also very good for showing up any surface imperfections, particularly on large flat areas such as tender and tank sides. It is sometimes suggested that this is also the best stage at which to fill cracks or blow holes in castings, and make good any other minor surface imperfections. Well, why not? I just prefer to ensure that as far as I can, I've eradicated all such blemishes before I start painting the model.

The primer can also be used as an undercoat to give a deeper, denser top coat under those colours which lack covering power. The various varieties of Crimson Lake immediately spring to mind, and here the usual grey primer should be replaced by red oxide. Crimson Lake paint of any make is generally translucent, and the use of a red oxide primer not only enables the top colour to cover more easily but makes for a much richer and denser final result. If red oxide as a primer is not available, a thin coat of LMS/LNER wagon bauxite or a similar red ochre shade can be used as an undercoat over grey primer.

I very rarely use the other primer colour, white, except when painting something which will have a very light coloured top coat. Refrigerator vans immediately come to mind, and if you have tried getting white paint to cover a dark undercoat you will know what I mean. White is not the easiest of colours to spray at the best of times, so any help you can give it is well worth-while.

I know that some modellers don't consider it necessary to prime models made from plastic, but I have to say that I think it is. However, care is essential if cellulose aerosol primers are used for this job. If applied too heavily, this paint has a nasty tendency to attack the plastic through the action of the cellulose solvent. The safe technique is to mist a couple of thin coats on, before putting a normal coat in place. However, the use of cellulose can now be avoided as Halfords have introduced 'Plastic Primer', sold for painting plastic bumpers and trim on cars. This is absolutely ideal for priming plastic models. The other class of primers - etching - is not suitable for plastic.

Which Primer?

By far the easiest way of priming a model is to use the spray cans of grey or red oxide cellulose primer sold for car touch-up work. My favourite brand is Holts Duplicolour, available from most motor accessory shops. Although somewhat wasteful of paint, they are by far the most convenient, and straightforward to use. There is now a new type of aerosol primer, available from chain DIY stores such as Do-It-All. Called Plasti-cote Super Primer, this is acetone based and at first try seems very good. I have only used it so far on one model, where it did the job as well as I would wish. It does seem to be thicker than other aerosol primers, though, so care will be needed.

Also available are the primers produced by the manufacturers of the paint we use to finish our models, and these should not be discounted. However, apart from Railmatch primer, these are not available in aerosol form, so the convenience of this sort of application is lost. Most of these paints are of the type known as etching primers, which as their name suggests actually etch into the surface of the metal to obtain a good bond. Their chemical action needs approximately

Two cans of aerosol primers - there are more........

twenty four hours to work satisfactorily.

Applying Primers

Obviously, aerosol primers are the easiest to apply. However, it's no good just giving the can a quick shake, spraying the model and expecting the primer to do its job. The instructions on the can recommend a minimum of two minutes vigorous shaking, and that's just what they need. Not just once, either; it's amazing how quickly the primer will settle back at the bottom of the can, requiring another good shaking to mix it properly again. Some modellers have told me that they spray this primer in to small air brush jars and then use the airbrush to prime the model. I have to say that I really don't see the point of this, unless it is to get the primer into some inaccessible areas. But I find those probably don't need much cover anyway.

Make sure you follow the manufacturers instructions and spray, for an even finish, at least 12" away from the subject.

All stages in the painting sequence are critical, but none more so than these first coats of primer. I aim for two applications to obtain coverage, with the first coat just light enough to show the metal underneath. Several thin coats are always much better than one thick one, for a number of reasons. As well as allowing much better control over the amount of paint being applied, nine times out of ten further applications will be necessary anyway. Although a single thick coat will generally cover most areas, other parts will be missed. Some filling in will invariably be needed, so to avoid excessive paint build up and the possibility of runs, light applications are best.

It is worth getting these first coats on whilst the model is still warm from the drying process, as water vapour is always present in the atmosphere to some extent. Spraying in warm, dry conditions will exclude as much of this as possible, as well as enabling the paint to dry just that bit quicker. Water vapour is one of the worst things for impairing paint adhesion - a good reason why spraying outside in the garage in damp conditions should be avoided at all costs.

If any further filling and rubbing down are felt to be necessary, now is the time to do this. However, unless you have missed something which requires drastic action, only the finest grades of wet and dry paper - from 600 grit downwards - should be used for rubbing down. If you have to go back to the metal for any reason, feather the edges of the paint around the offending patch with the wet and dry. Done this way, once the model is re-coated with primer no sign of the repair will show. The coarsest of these fine grades, 600 grit, is used at the start of this process, finishing off with a piece of fairly well worn 1000. If there is a large area to be rubbed down, try Evo-Stiking the paper to thin balsa wood and using this as a rubbing stick. There will then be little chance of making a hollow in the surface by rubbing too hard with the fingers.

All this rubbing-down work should be done 'in the wet', as it were. I fill a bowl with lukewarm water, with a touch of washing up liquid added. This not only helps to keep the paper from clogging up, but gives a smoother finish to the surface. Constantly washing the paper during rubbing down ensures that the residue from the paint or filler will be removed as progress is made. And, of course, when the repair business has been finished the model will need another wash to remove any residue. Such an intermediate wash, followed by thorough drying, is no bad thing, especially if the model is left for any time between priming and painting.

Undercoats

Colours used as undercoats will affect the look of the top coat, as already noted. An appropriate undercoat can be used to *change* the appearance of a top coat - this was often done on the prototype in pre-grouping days. As many of you will know - if you didn't it probably shows in many of the photographs used - I am quite an enthusiast for the North Eastern Railway. Now, there is some debate within the NER modelling fraternity about the colour the coaches were painted, a shade of Crimson Lake similar to that used by the Midland, research suggesting that it was a darker shade than the latter, although personally I don't subscribe to that view. However, to achieve such a darker shade of this basic colour, a thin coat of dark blue over the primer followed by the top coat will give the required effect. The blue showing through gives a deeper, darker hue to the crimson lake, making it appear subtly different. The same technique can be used to influence any sort of top coats. The method I use for painting Gresley coaches depends on a variation of just this technique, on which more later.

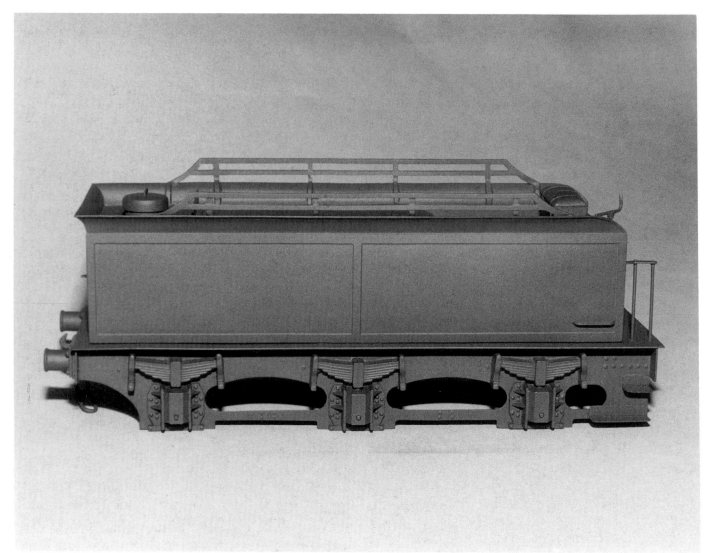

The red prime alternative. As the top coat is to be Crimson Lake, the undercoat needs to match.

Chapter Four

THE AIRBRUSH

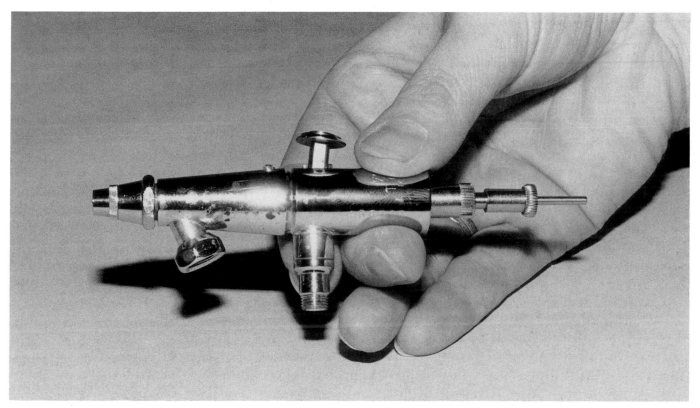

The PAASCHE VL Double action inside admission air brush. In design very similar to other double action brushes such as the Badger 150 - see below. The knurled knob at the rear holds the needle in place as it tightens onto a tapered bearing. This is about as big as an airbrush gets, of this type, and in my opinion is about the best on the market.

The airbrush has always been an important instrument for the graphic artist, and with modern production methods and techniques, has become a relatively cheap tool for the modelmaker. Since the early part of this century, when the airbrush was first invented, it has been developed to a degree which would astonish those early pioneers. The versatile brushes now available are capable of producing some of the most complex work. Whilst we are concerned mainly with the relatively simple business of projecting paint at model railway equipment, an airbrush catalogue such as Badger's will show just what can be done with some of the more sophisticated brushes.

The principle on which the airbrush works is really very simple. One of the basic laws of physics states that if air is blown across the top of an open tube, the atmospheric pressure at the top of the tube will be lowered. Obviously, if the bottom of this tube is immersed in a liquid on which full atmospheric pressure is acting, then that liquid will be drawn to the top of the tube by the resulting pressure difference. If the air is blown across the top of the tube with sufficient force, the liquid will not only be sucked up, but will also be atomised. Although the resulting spray would go everywhere in the case of an open tube, if the tube is enclosed in a nozzle the spray can be directed. This is the basic principle of all spraying equipment.

Airbrush Types

Basically, there are two different types of airbrush: external mix and internal mix. External mix brushes combine the air and paint outside the airbrush head, and produce a slightly coarser spray pattern, while internal mix brushes produce a smoother pattern by bringing the air and paint together inside the spraying head. Internal mix brushes can also be sub-

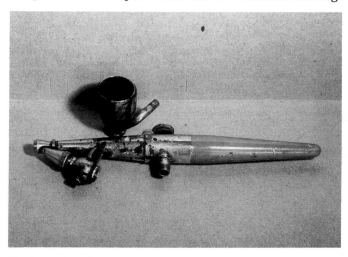

My favourite all round air brush, the PAASCHE 'H' - outside mix, very simple with a rugged construction.

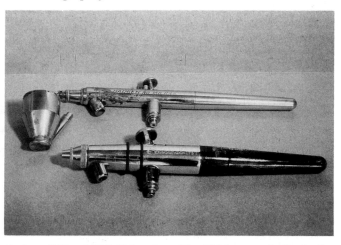

Badger 150 and 175 Airbrushes. The 175 is *very* similar to the PAASCHE VL, but not in my opinion quite as good. I use the 150 for detail work such as weathering and touch up.

divided into two main categories, single and dual action. These descriptions relate to the trigger action of the airbrush. In a 'single action' brush, there are two separate controls. The trigger in this case simply regulates the amount of air being drawn through the brush. The flow of paint is determined by a screw at the end of the handle, which controls the position of the needle in the 'jet' of the nozzle. A 'dual action' brush, on the other hand, has only one control for both paint and air. The trigger on top of the brush has a dual movement, being pressed down for air, and then pulled back for paint, giving much finer and more responsive control. This type of brush is obviously the most sophisticated and thus, of course, the most expensive.

Choosing an Airbrush

Which brush should you choose when looking at all the different types and makes on the market? Over the past few years, since becoming a full time professional modelmaker, I have tried various types of brushes from several different manufacturers. Most of them perform very well, within the constraints of the different designs and the uses for which they are intended. So the choice of a brush will come down to two things:what you want to do with it, and how much you want to spend.

As far as I can determine, the cheapest airbrush on the market at the moment is the Badger 250, which at the time of writing costs around £10. It is, understandably, relatively crude and basically blows air across a tube in a jar full of thinned paint. This results in a very wide spray pattern which wastes quite a lot of paint. However, if care is taken good results can be obtained. At that price, who can afford not to have a try?

Next up the scale of sophistication and price is the single action outside admission type of brush, such as the Paasche 'H' or Badger 350. The Paasche is a good, well made brush, selling for about £50, while the Badger, a very similar design but nowhere near as robust, costs around £30. Both brushes can be adapted to spray anything from light inks and water colours to heavier enamels and high viscosity materials, simply by changing needle and valve cone assemblies.

In the ranges of airbrushes easily available, only Badger, so far as I know, make a single action internal mix type, their model 200. At a current price of approximately £45, this is understandably very popular amongst modellers, and with practice will give results comparable to those achieved by a dual-action brush.

This leaves the Badger 100 and 150 and Paasche V and VL double action brushes. Both of these makes have interchangeable head and needle assemblies to spray anything from light materials in lines a sixteenth of an inch wide to broad swathes of heavier flu-

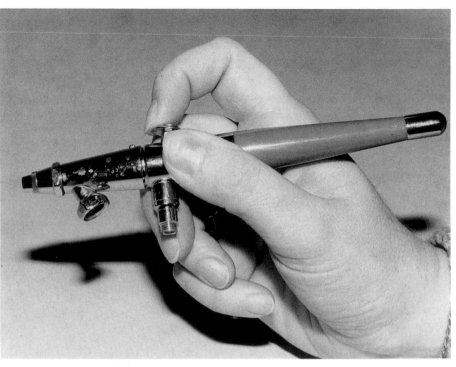

Re PAASCHE VL in use. Push the trigger down for air, and pull back for paint.

ids such as acrylics and ceramic glazes. These sophisticated and versatile brushes are the most expensive, with prices reaching over a hundred pounds for the top models.

Recommended Choices

It is obviously not possible to analyse in detail all the different airbrushes available on the market. Those I have mentioned above are particularly suitable for our hobby, but reference to the various manufacturers' catalogues will give a good idea of what can be bought, often for much more esoteric work than we could envisage. Generally, airbrushes by different manufacturers are pretty much the same in operation, the differences coming in quality and versatility. For model work, where the brush is really only being used as a miniature precision spray gun, it really comes down to what you can afford to pay. I am firmly of the opinion that when buying tools of any description you should go for quality; it is always worth paying that little bit extra for it.

Given that all we need to achieve is a smooth, even paint surface, with good coverage and easy application, it doesn't necessarily follow that the more you pay for an airbrush the better the result will be. In some instances, the more sophisticated brushes don't allow enough paint to be sprayed on quickly enough, which can result in an uneven finish. This does not happen too often in 4mm scale and below, I'm pleased to say, but in 7mm and above the much greater areas to be covered can cause problems.

Of the more basic brushes, the single action external mix Paasche 'H' is exceptionally good. With its interchangeable head assemblies, it will cope with most spraying jobs and is extremely easy to maintain and keep

clean. However, where it does lose a bit of refinement is in the spray pattern, which is of a large dot or coarse pattern. Among the simple internal mix brushes, the Badger 200 is as good as you will find, and gains on the Paasche with its finer, small dot spray pattern. More care is, however, needed in maintenance. Cleaning is more difficult because the paint and air is mixed inside the body of the brush, where it is harder to get at.

I also have in my possession a Badger 150. This is a slightly more sophisticated type than the Badger 200, in that it is a dual action brush. At a cost currently of around £85. This is a brush which some modellers may well consider; through the control available it is more versatile, being suitable not just for locomotives and rolling stock but for other applications such as scenic work. The same is true of a recent introduction by Richard Khonstam's, who now import the Badger range. The Badger 175 Crescendo is similar in operation to the 150, but has a much more 'chunky' feel to it. The needle and valve assemblies are a lot bigger, and it seems that it will be possible to spray greater quantities and heavier materials with it.

For 7mm scale and above, it may become necessary to use a spray gun rather than an airbrush, due to the sheer quantity of paint involved. The guns are smaller versions of those used to spray the family car, and can normally be bought from motor trade paint suppliers. One gun which I know to be good and reliable is the De Vilbiss type MP, which at the time of writing costs around £160. These guns are capable of spraying much heavier liquids, such as cellulose, and in enough quantity to avoid uneven finishes. Not unnaturally, a larger compressor is required to power them, and can be had from the same sources.

Strangely, the only airbrush which I have tried, and at length, but cannot recommend, is the De Vilbiss Sprite. It is, by a long way, the cheapest of the double action brushes, but it seems very much to be made to a price. When it is working, the action is very good, but its reliability is, in my experience, rather suspect. I have tried two, and both let me down. Perhaps I was unlucky, but I'm inclined to doubt it. However, I have spoken to other modellers who use this type of brush, and they tell me that they have got on with them very well.

Each to his own, say I.

Barnfield's Bouquet

Thinking about the various airbrushes I either own or have tried at length, I have to say that the relatively inexpensive Paasche 'H', although not apparently as sophisticated as, say, the Badger 150 or 200, is as good an all round brush as we modellers are likely to need. It is simple, rugged, easily cleaned and maintained. It lasts well, too; mine must be getting on for its Silver Jubilee by now. Inevitably, bits will wear out, and I have replaced

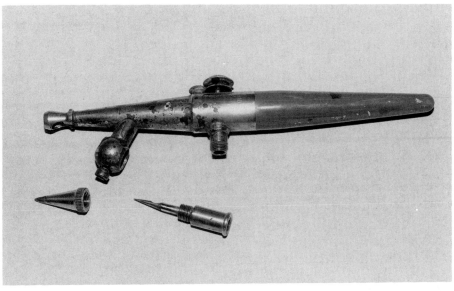

The PAASCHE 'H' in pieces. This shows just how simple this type of brush is to keep clean.

the nozzle and tip assembly in the last few years. But that's not a bad record, considering some of the 'hammer' it's had in that time. I think it is fair to say that over the years I have frequently put the Paasche

ABOVE: Power Unit. BELOW: Micron air compressor, complete with pressure gauge and moisture trap. The knob on the top regulates the pressure.

to one side to use one or other of the many alternative brushes on the market, but so far I have always come back to it. It performs all that is asked of it.

Propellants for Airbrushing

Now we have established that the airbrush is the tool for us, how do we make best use of it, and what propellant do we use to get the paint from its container, on to the model? Basically, there are four ways of propelling the paint in the desired direction. The two most common are the pressurised propellant cans sold by most of the airbrush manufacturers, or compressed air from either a stored source or a mechanical compressor.

All the airbrush suppliers provide an adaptor to fit the airline to a car tyre, but it's not a good idea to use the spare from your car for this as the constant inflation and deflation could damage the tyre. However, a scrap rim and tyre will provide clean air for airbrush propulsion, if in a rather cumbersome form. Lugging the thing down to the local garage or pumping it up with a foot pump does not sound like fun to me! An inner tube on its own might be a better bet if you don't inflate it too hard. Much more civilised is a suitable small compressor, once again usually supplied by the airbrush manufacturer.

The fourth option we have is to use CO_2 gas cylinders. These are good if you do a lot of spraying but the noise is a nuisance. The cylinders are very heavy and difficult to move about, while the initial outlay, to cover the deposit on the cylinder, may be considered excessive. By the time cylinder rental has been taken into account, this outlay is probably more than halfway towards the cost of a small compressor. Some sort of regulator will also be required, and may not be easy to find. The last drawback is, of course, that large amounts of CO_2 wafting around can give you a headache or worse, so once again the extractor booth is a must.

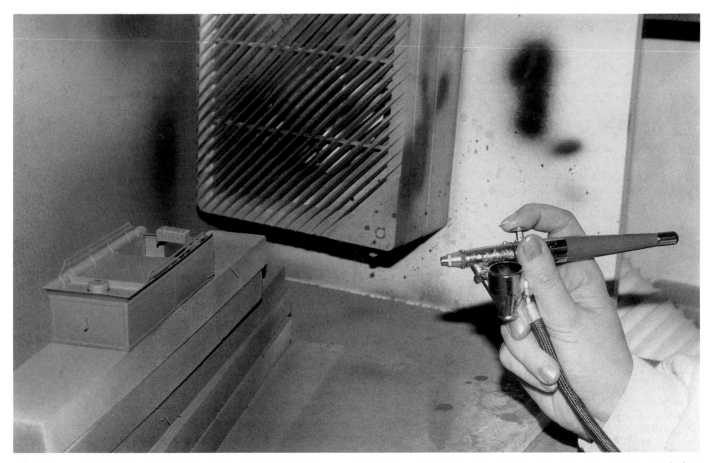

How to go airbrushing. Hold at about shoulder height, finger on the trigger. Note the size of the extractor fan. This is needed to remove as much paint and fumes as possible, venting to the atmoshere by means of a flexible pipe as used in tumble driers.

The two best options for us are propellant cans or a small compressor. The cans come in various sizes, and for those who will use the airbrush only two or three times a year they will suffice and be economical. A word of warning here, though:the propellant can run out at the most inappropriate moments, so if a paint job is about to be undertaken, make sure there is sufficient available to see you through to the finish. If in doubt, change the can before you start.

For the modeller who sprays a number of models a year, a compressor becomes an absolute boon. It will soon pay for itself, not only in monetary terms where you have been buying lots of propellant cans, but in sheer convenience. Compressors of the type we need to power the airbrush are readily available, the cheapest at around £100. When I was at the stage of getting to paint more than the odd model or two for John Fowler, these small compressors were not as easily available as they are now and were comparatively expensive. As I seemed to be getting through rather a lot of cans, I was relieved when John came to the rescue, supplying my first compressor in exchange for my painting a model for him.

My current compressor also came to me by way of exchange, this time against an article in *Model Railways* magazine. It is a Micon, readily available from Badger stockists, and highly suitable for use with airbrushes. I have added a one piece air filter, a pressure gauge and a moisture trap, which ensures that the air reaching the brush is clean and dry. The output pressure is very easy to govern, with a single knob for control. I also have a second unit, very old, as a standby. This has been rebuilt with an arm and diaphragm from yet another old compressor after the bearings in the cam finally gave out, at a time when I didn't fancy spending a lot of money on a new unit. It is very noisy, and so only gets used in emergencies or if I need the two on together.

Basic Airbrush Techniques

With the airbrush linked up to a propellent source, you can now get to the point when you press the trigger and air comes through the brush for the first time. Before trying to spray any paint, add some thinners, or even cold water, to the cup or bottle and experiment with the brush characteristics. If you're using thinners, even white spirit (which is actually quite noxious stuff), then heed the precautions outlined in Chapter 1. Ensure you've got good ventilation and don the spray mask.

If possible, hold the brush at arm's length in the light and spray at right angles to your line of sight. By moving the needle or nozzle back and forth you will get a good idea of the spray pattern of your brush. The main object in trying out an airbrush for the first time is to get the 'feel' of it, and the best way of doing this is to find the minimum and maximum lines that the brush can produce. Try spraying onto white or light coloured card pinned at about shoulder height to a vertical surface. Depending on the type of brush you have chosen, you will need to vary the air pressure through the trigger and the flow through either the trigger or regulator screw. Playing around with these generally will help you explore the characteristics inherent in the brush.

Once you are happy with the basic brush characteristics, move on to spraying some paint onto the test card. When spraying, always keep the brush moving and start to spray just before hitting the card. Keep the brush moving parallel with the card, and stop spraying when the jet of paint has passed the edge of the card. In this way you will get accustomed to using the brush and will also gain an idea of your own skill. Before moving on to actually spray a model, it will also pay to experiment with paint consistency, and to get to know better whether you have mixed it too thin or too thick. If it is too thick it will be drying as it comes out of the nozzle, and will create a fuzzy effect on the card. If too thin, it will start to run before covering. It is a simple matter to add either paint or thinners to the mix until it is just right, and the card can be covered evenly. Once the general characteristics of the airbrush and paint mixtures have been mastered, try painting an old plastic wagon body as a trial piece, to get an idea of how paint goes onto a model and what it will look like when it has been correctly sprayed.

With the practice from experimenting in this way, you will soon gain confidence and feel able to tackle something more ambitious. You know, those half-finished kits that have been sitting on the shelf, the ones you have hesitated to paint for fear that a bad job would spoil the model. Have confidence, and if you proceed with patience and step by step, you will soon develop your airbrush skills to the point where you will never want to consider brush painting a model, ever again!

Don't Forget the Weather

Actual conditions for spraying are, I feel, as important as anything else, and extremes of heat and cold will certainly affect how the paint dries. Although the phrase 'room temperature' can cover quite a wide latitude, comfortable indoor temperatures of around 65 - 70 degrees Fahrenheit are pretty well ideal. Most paints have quite a large temperature range in which good results can be obtained, but there are limits. Spraying in conditions that are too cold results in very uneven drying, while if conditions are too hot the paint will go off too quickly, with the thinners evaporating before the paint has flowed out, leading to the pigments drying thick and treacly.

Cleaning the Airbrush

Of course, once you have used paint through your airbrush it will need to be cleaned, and this seems to be one aspect that puts many people off using airbrushes. When I've been demonstrating at exhibitions, the one question which keeps cropping up is "Oh yes, that's all very well, but how do you keep it clean?" The basic rule here is to clean the brush *as soon as you have finished using it.* The first part to tackle is the jar or cup. Any paint left should be rinsed out with thinners, and once this has been done, some neat thinners are sprayed through the gun until no trace of paint is left. Next, withdraw the needle and, with a cotton bud dipped in thinners, clean the nozzle so that any build up of paint is removed. That, really, is it and once you get into the habit, it will become second nature.

Periodically - perhaps when each model is completed - refer to the airbrush instruction book and remove the needle and nozzle assembly. Gently clean all the surfaces of these with another cotton bud soaked in thinners. A useful product available from some airbrush stockists is an aerosol cleaner called Spray - Away. This is formulated not only to help clean the brush, but also to lubricate it by means of an additive. This will keep the needle and other parts moving freely.

Having thus considered in some detail the choice, use and care of our main painting tool, we must now consider the important matter of the paint we intend to use in it.

Right : 4 - Airbrush cleaner also contains a small amount of lubricant to keep things moving nicely.

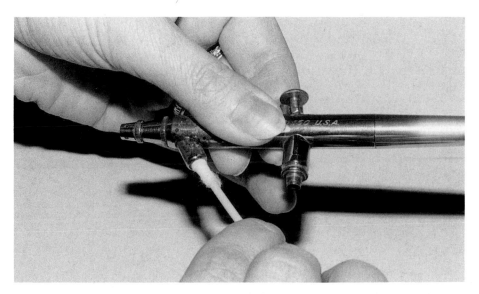

Cleaning the brush after use. A cotton wool bud moistened with thinners pushed through - 1. The paint inlet.

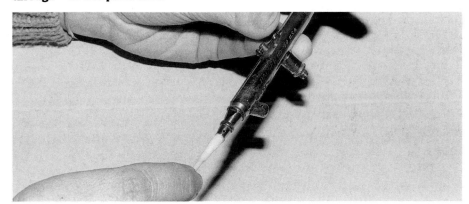

2 - In the outlet

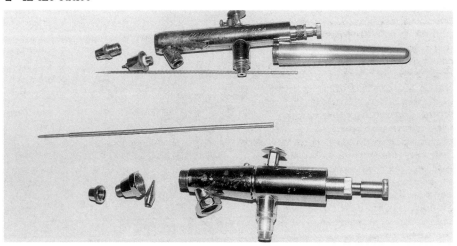

3 - Dismantle all parts and clean thoroughly with thinners and wipe with a cloth.

Chapter Five

PAINTS AND THINNERS

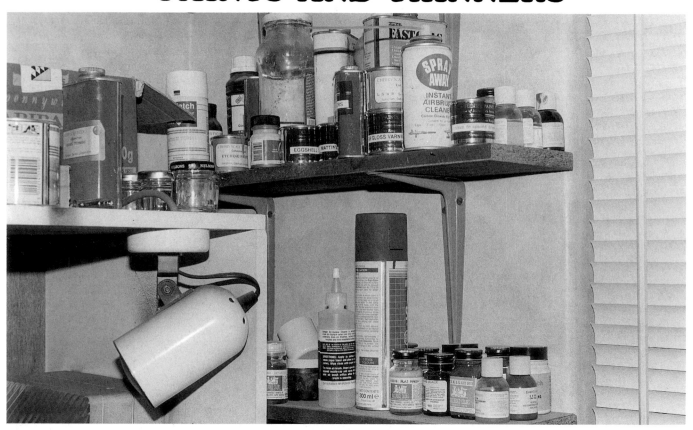

A bit of a hotchpotch here. Lots of paints, thinners and other sundry items all ready and close to hand. Floquil, Cherry, Railmatch - you name it, its probably amongst this lot.

Having discussed both the airbrush and its means of propulsion, time now for a word or two about the paint we shall be putting through it. Paint is complex stuff, but is basically composed of a carrier, usually some form of varnish, and a mixture of pigments which determine the colour. These days, there will also be all sorts of additives to give it this or that property. The carrier varnish is usually some form of resin in solution in a solvent base, the same solvent generally being used to thin the paint to the desired consistency for brushing or spraying. Matt paints also contain matting agents, usually in the form of a fine powder or paste mixed into the varnish. Matting agents are often opaque, and for this reason tend to dull the colours slightly.

The Modeller's Enamel Paint Ranges

Until fairly recently, the two most popular ranges available to the railway modeller have been Humbrol and Precision. Both have marketed a large range of colours in specialist modelling areas, while Humbrol have a good selection of more general colours in both gloss and matt finishes. Both these ranges are oil based enamels, and are available from most model railway and many general model shops throughout the British Isles. These enamels are readily thinned with their

If only I had a pound for every tin of Humbrol paint I've used over the years. This paint must have been the most popular used by railway modellers until only very recently.

'own brand' thinners, or with white spirit. If you must have the best, you can go one better and use pure turpentine. Both ranges have had their paints and varnishes available in small spray cans, which are useful when an airbrush is not available.

Viewed as a paint, rather than being judged on the quality or accuracy of the colours, I have found Humbrol

to be the best on the market for model use. It has come in for a lot of criticism over the years, mainly because of what seemed to be a lack of research in the formulation of the railway colours. Unfortunately, some of these *were* totally wrong, but many others were only a shade or two out. Unfortunately, a few of the colours were also very 'muddy', and when ap-

Some of the successors to Humbrol. Cherry Paints, excellent. In my opinion the best enamel type paint available.

plied looked awful. Maybe these problems are the reason why the railway colours have been withdrawn.

Until very recently, the quality of Humbrol paint was excellent. Nowadays, it is not quite as good as it was - I suspect a new formula, probably intended to make the paint more user friendly. The new mix came in at about the same time as the tinlet numbers were all changed, and if not quite what it once was, is nonetheless still as good as the competition, whether brushing or spraying.

The trouble Humbrol had with its railway colours brought Precision and others into the market. The covering power of Precision paints does sometimes leave a bit to be desired, particularly the reds and maroons, but with a good undercoat they will cover adequately and come out looking right. At the moment Precision Paints are going through a supply problem: basically, at the time of writing (summer 1993), they were not being made. The wholesalers, W & H Models, assured me that (at the time) they held good stocks of many of the colours in the range.

Newer Ranges

A newer range of oil based paints are the Cherry Paints, supplied by Micrologica Systems. With the virtual demise of Precision, Cherry Paints have made a conscious decision to supply the needs of railway modellers who are more interested in the steam era. As yet, they are not supplying their paints in aerosol form, but I suspect these may come. The Cherry range is now quite extensive, with over 140 different colours available, though not all are intended for the railway modeller; some are for people who model other forms of transport. Most of the range is supplied in a gloss finish, intended to facilitate the easy application of waterslide transfers. Personally, I prefer an eggshell type of finish to the paint, with a final varnish to control the gloss.

Cherry do, however, supply a very good matting agent for those like me who like to take the paint away from full gloss down towards eggshell. This matting agent really is excellent, being a liquid rather than a paste. In the past, some paints have suffered when being matted down by the manufacturers (as described in the introduction) where a white paste - often talc - is added. This affected the paint colour rendition, making the shade appear rather duller or paler than it really was. The Cherry matting agent is a virtually clear liquid, but quite concentrated - in the tin it looks like a rather thick varnish. In their usage notes, which they will send to the modeller on application, Cherry provide a list of do's and dont's, amongst which are the mixing ratios needed to matt the paint down. As with other enamels, care is needed when thinning for spraying, and once again the appropriate ratios are advised. Cherry paints are a real joy to spray, with either their own thinners or with xylene.

Another paint range of relatively recent origin comes from Railmatch. This is also oil-based and sprays very well. The range was originally biased more toward the current scene, but does now include a number of colours for the steam enthusiast. Most of these are post-grouping colours for the 'Big 4' 1923 - 48 period, with only a few suited to pre-grouping railways. In addition to all the railway liveries there are a number of more 'general' shades, such as signal red and a selection of weathering colours, along with various varnishes and metallic paints.

I have to say that I have not had a lot of experience with Railmatch, but talking to other modellers who have, it seems that it will be suitable for my methods. However, I am also told that quality does sometimes seem to vary, with shades sometimes changing from batch to batch. Thinning for spraying is also quite critical, with little leeway between too thick and too thin. Ratio Plastic Models have very kindly donated some of their Midland Railway coach sides for me to play around with for this book, and I have sprayed a pair of them with Railmatch Midland Crimson. Although I got on with it reasonably well, I found it rather unforgivably. The covering power was perfectly adequate over a red oxide undercoat. As an aside, why do Railmatch include the words 'For Professional Model Makers Only' on their jars? To get around some regulation, perhaps.

Floquil; Late Lamented of the USA

A favourite paint which until very recently has been available for our use

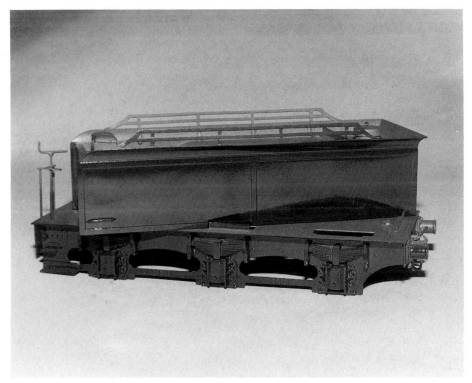

Cherry Paints give a rich, deep, glossy finish, which I tone down with an eggshell varnish.

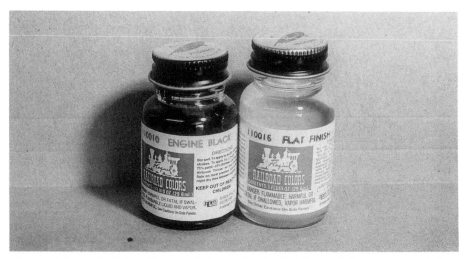

The much lamented Floquil range. Quite the best paint for modellers until overtaken by events and safety considerations, but still used extensively in the good old U.S. of A. Quite why it hasn't been withdrawn is somewhat of a mystery considering their predilection for safety in other areas.

is Floquil, imported from the USA by Victors. Floquil is not oil or cellulose based, but uses xylene, an industrial solvent. As already noted in Chapter 1, there are some drawbacks associated with xylene, which needs treating with respect. As a paint, however, I can say that Floquil was probably the best for small scale models ever available in this country. Covering capacity is excellent, and at £1.60 per 1 fl. oz. bottle, represented very good value for money. Although the colours were formulated mainly for the American market, their Engine Black, together with weathering colours and varnishes, were very good.

I have to write in the past tense, as currently Floquil, along with many other paints containing flammable and toxic solvents such as xylene, cannot be shipped to this country by air. Shipping by sea is only suited to bulk consignments, is far more expensive and takes too long. Even I must concede that a whole 40-foot container full of Floquil would be rather too much of a good thing! To me, this loss is a real pity. In my opinion, it was the best paint available to modellers, and if I had my way in an ideal world, would use Floquil to paint everything.

Cellulose Paints

When writing about paints for model work, it is sometimes easy to forget the vast range of paints available to the modeller that are actually intended for the motor trade. Go into a branch of Halfords, or any other motor accessory shop, and there are racks of aerosol spray cans of cellulose touch-up paint in all manner of colours and shades. Many modellers have used 'BMC Damask Red', from what is now the Rover group but was once the British Motor Corporation, for Midland and LMS crimson Lake. Personally, I think the shade is a little too dark, but as already established, you pays your money and takes your choice on that one.

Then there are the custom suppli-

regarded just because they're not actually *called* LNER Green or LMS Crimson. With some perseverance, matches can be found. For instance, I have used Tamiya Dark Sea Grey No. XF54 for NER Wagon Grey. It's a dead ringer for the shade once sold by Precision, which is no longer available. I am sure there are other such matches to be found. Humbrol also have their range of 'Acrylic Hobby Paints' to complement their enamels, but for some reason these don't seem to be stocked by some model shops.

The big snag with most acrylics is that, unlike enamel based paints, they have no inherent ingredients which harden on drying. This leaves the acrylic surface rather soft and somewhat prone to the 'rubbing off' effect. A good varnish, however, will normally prevent this. Victor's, the one-time

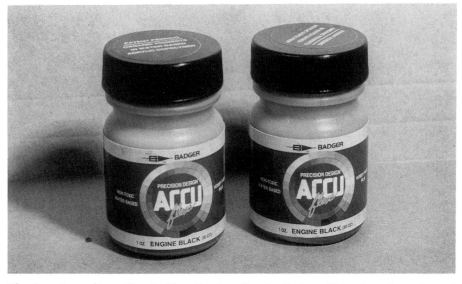

The American alternative to Floquil - Accuflex by Badger. Water based acrylic and non-toxic.

ers to the motor trade. Here in Peterborough, for instance, I know of at least three, so try your Yellow Pages. They have literally thousands of paint samples to choose from, and even if the particular shade you want is not one of them, they can mix something to your satisfaction while you wait. The only snag is that you have to buy in minimum quantities of half a litre, which paints an awful lot of models. But I think it is well worth the expense to get the exact shade of paint you want. These paints should also be cellulose based, so make sure they don't mix you a modern 2-pack isocyanate, which is lovely stuff but lethal without the right spraying gear.

Acrylics

Another type of paint which has been largely ignored by the model railway hobby is the acrylic. As noted in Chapter 1, these are becoming increasingly popular in the USA, while over here military modellers have been using them for years. Again, there are lots of different colours, available in a number of ranges. None to my knowledge are made to suit railway prototype colours, but they shouldn't be dis-

importers of Floquil, are now stocking a paint new to this country, 'Accu-Flex'. This is noted in my first chapter as being popular in the USA, where it is being marketed by Badger Airbrushes. It is a water based acrylic paint, made with high quality automotive grade organic pigments. Being water based, it has a non-toxic solvent.

Like Floquil, Accu-Flex colours have been formulated for the American market, but I'm sure there will be some which will be useful to the British modeller. The importers of Badger products, Richard Khonstam Ltd., have helpfully sent me some of this paint to try, and it certainly seems to be useful. It is claimed, both on the bottle and in the promotional material, that no primer is necessary, though I have my doubts about this. In my initial trials, it certainly seems to cling very well to unprimed brass - though brass is notorious for paint adhesion failing after some time has passed, so we shall see. On primed surfaces, though, it really does seem to stick. It may be that Badger have solved the problems inherent with acrylics and Accu-Flex paint has certainly received some glowing reports in the US modelling press.

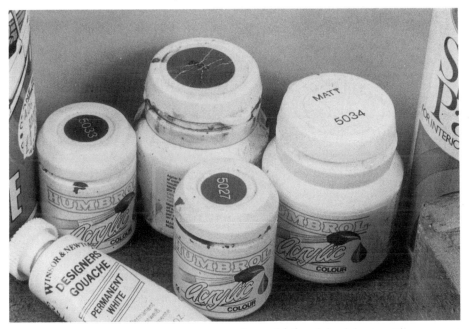

Other Paint Types

There are, of course, many other paints available for use on our models. But as this book is concerned with painting and lining locomotives and rolling stock, water colours, poster paints, gouache, and so on are not really relevant. The products listed and described above are those that I have found suitable for such work using my painting methods.

Thinners and Paint Preparation

All the paint manufacturers sell thinners for their paints, but to my mind this is a very expensive way of thinning paint. Not only are these "own brand' thinners sold only in small cans, but often they are only a common solvent such as white spirit. As this can be bought on any high street, at a much lower price in sensible-size containers, I see no point in buying the paintmakers 'own brands'. The paint manufacturers will tell you, of course, that there are this and that additive in their thinners, but I've never found any difference in use, apart perhaps from a slight variation in drying times. This is so small as to be negligible.

Short drying times are a good idea,

to avoid the risk of dust settling on wet paint. I have found that drying times can be usefully reduced by thinning paints with xylene. The various risks associated with powerful organic solvents like this have already been discussed in Chapter 1, and if the precautions set out there are carefully observed, then this combination of paint and thinner makes for excellent results. Don't forget that many thinners, including xylene, cellulose and ordinary white spirit, are skin irritants. I have already mentioned the use of disposable surgical gloves when handling a cleaned model, and they can also be used when mixing paints to avoid getting thinners on the hands.

I first came across xylene as a thinner when Mike Skidmore introduced me to Floquil paints, which are xylene based. It was at this time I discovered how expensive 'in house' thinners could be. That for Floquil, Dio-Sol, is pure xylene, and was sold in 5 fl.oz. bottles, each costing about £3.50. By contrast, last time I bought five litres of xylene it cost about £8.50. A few sums tell me that this puts the cost of Dio-Sol at £0.70 a fluid ounce, and xylene at less than a penny for the same amount!

Xylene will thin any of the enamels

on the market, and will also significantly reduce the drying time. I now use it for thinning all enamels as well as Floquil. It is currently obtainable from good pharmacutical chemists, although they may well want to know what you want it for. Given that it is toxic, and that many new regulations on such materials are coming in, it may not continue to be so freely available. When buying from your chemist, be sure to specify pure xylene, as it is available with additives.

More often than not it is necessary to dilute our spraying paints, with the appropriate thinner. I prefer to do this in separate airtight jars, transferring the paint at the right consistency to the airbrush cup or bottle. In this way, thinned paint is not wasted, and can be kept in storage ready to spray when the next job in that colour comes along. It is difficult to give a definitive answer as to the extent paint should be thinned. Some makes need more than others, indeed some colours from the same range of paints differ in the amount of thinning they need. Suffice it to say that the consistency for spraying should be something like pouring cream. That is, not as thin as milk, but thinner than double cream...

Paint preparation starts by stirring your tin of paint thoroughly - this requires some sort of broad based implement, such as a lolly stick, for about four to five minutes. Alternatively, you could invest in a mechanical paint mixer, such as the American Robart paint shaker, which is battery operated. This thorough stirring is more important with matt paints, for if all the matting agent is not mixed a streaky finish could result. Once the mixing is complete, pour about one quarter of the tinlet (I'm assuming the usual 15ml. Humbrol or Precision size) into your mixing jar.

With an eye dropper, add to the paint approximately one quarter the amount in thinners, ie, 75% paint, 25% thinners. Put on the bottle cap and shake well to mix the two together, and have a look at the result. In general, if the thinned paint has covered the inside of the lid and does not run away, the consistency is about right. However, it may still be too thick for spraying, and the only way to tell is to try it. This is where a little bit of practice comes in, and it is now worth testing your airbrush with actual paint mix. Should the spray consistency be wrong, this can be adjusted by adding small amounts of paint or thinner.

Only a small amount of the thinned paint should be transferred to your airbrush cup or bottle. I prefer using a side cup on the airbrush, not only because it is easy to keep clean, but less paint is wasted and it is possible to adjust the paint mix in the cup. With the paint mixed, thinned and passing properly through the brush, *you* are ready to start spraying a model.

Some people use the strangest things to finish their models! This selection is down to Iain Rice.

Chapter Six

PAINTING TECHNIQUES

Spray-Painting

Having discussed in some detail the means and the materials needed, now is the time to start actually painting something. Initially, what is wanted is a test piece, much as suggested in the airbrush familiarisation routine set out in Chapter 4. Most model shops have something suitable second hand, and for a small outlay you can purchase, say, an old plastic wagon body. It doesn't really matter what state it is in, so long as it will serve as an advanced practice piece. The idea is to develop a successful technique on something that doesn't matter, so that you can learn about the pitfalls and discover the strengths and limitations of your spraying set-up.

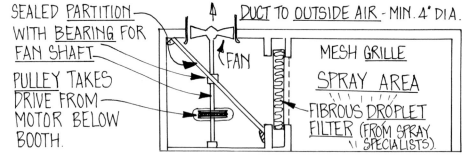

Test piece or no, you won't learn much unless the item is properly prepared for spraying. So, I'm afraid, you will have to remove old paint and lettering, and generally clean up the model so that it is in a suitable "raw state". Getting the old paint off these bodies can sometimes be a real pain - see the section on paint stripping in Chapter 2 - so you may prefer to practice on something like a cheap plastic wagon kit, which will give you a clean start.

Assuming that the test piece is a plastic body, it should ideally be primed with a suitable primer. Obviously, the best thing is to use one of the acrylic primers formulated for plastic, but if you haven't been able to find one, don't

worry too much, and have a go on the unprimed plastic. It is, however, just as important to have the test piece as clean as if it were a 'proper' model, so it is worth going through the various appropriate cleaning stages. It is also worth remembering that plastic can accumulate a certain amount of static electricity, which will attract dust. However, if you follow the normal washing methods of cleaning and do not rub the model dry with a cloth or tissue paper, then this should not be a problem.

If you are priming, heed the advice given in the section on primers, and apply several thin coats of paint. Each light coat of primer should be given a

few minutes to dry before applying the next, until the whole of the model is covered. It is important not to get too much paint in any one place. By pausing between coats, it is easy to see if excess paint is tending to accumulate in particular places. Give them a miss on the next pass of the airbrush. If you are anything like me your first attempt will not be that satisfactory, but it is well worth persevering, even if you have to wash off the offending paint and start again. As with so many other things, in using an airbrush practice makes perfect.

Once the model has been primed, some colour can be applied. Primers normally take very little time to dry,

NER Class A 2-4-2T in pristine livery. Personally I think too much polished metalwork on a model locomotive sometimes looks wrong. Model built by Steve Ross.

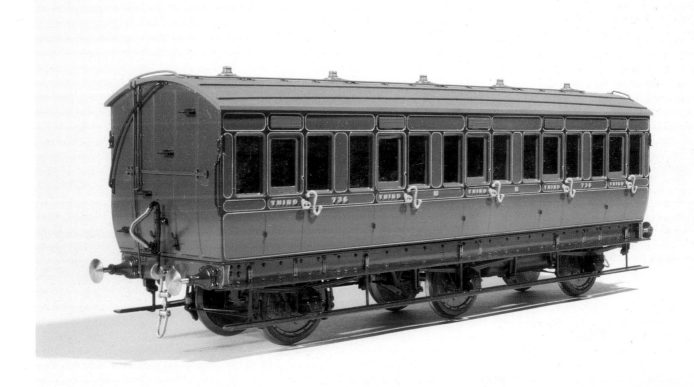

A superb Slaters 6 wheel MR all third carriage. Here is a case where I disagree with the manufacturer, who suggest fixing the body to the chassis and leaving the roof removable. I fixed the roof and made the body screw to the chassis making the painting a little easier. As on the prototype the beading on the model is curved and not flat - it is therefor important to get the lines in the right place.

The Alan Gibson Kit of a Lynton and Barnstaple 2-6-2T. Building and painting something like this is very satisfying, as 7mm narrow gauge can sometimes be more of a challenge and so more interesting.

The DJH A1 Kit alongside Proscales A3. Of the 'two' colour liveries, LNER Green can be the most difficult - lining around cabs, windows and washout plugs calls for extra care to ensure accuracy.

Two locomotives for 'Bramblewick'. NER Class N and O, both John Redrups, at London Road Models. They are amongst the best kits for the NER modeller.

LNWR Cauliflower 0-6-0; again a superb London Road Models Kit, built by John Hayes for Mike Peascod, Chairman of the Scale Four Society.

NER 4-wheeled all third kit from my own range.

Rising Star N2 Kit with much added detail as specified by the customer. LNER lined black is a particular favourite of mine.

Two views of my favourite model and prototype. It started off as a Model Loco Kit and has been converted to P4 standards with lots of detail added.

LNER V2 Class No.4774. This was my first big scratch-built loco and was done really as a bit of a challenge. If I was doing it now I would probably make a few changes. At the time I built it, c.1980, I had the idea that one loco from every class shedded at New England would be nice. The P1 illustrated later was the second of the grand plan.

This ex-LMS coach shows just how effective two colour livery can be if it is done properly. This is the correct version - see the section on masking for the incorrect version. It is very easy to get things wrong if you don't do your research properly.

Two views of the superb Bramblewick layout featuring (top) a Class P and (lower) a Class B both subtly weathered by Tom Harland. The P was a bit of a trial as the kit is very poor. However, the B ,ex-George Norton and now London Road Models, was as good as was the former poor. Photographs courtesey BARRY NORMAN

Mustn't forget the contemporary scene represented here by a 47 and an 86 kitted out in Network South East livery. Both models built and painted by Dave Lowery.

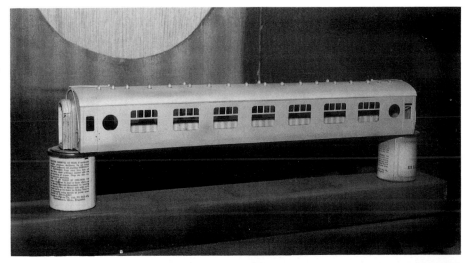

suppliers. In an emergency, ordinary Sellotape can be used, provided the adhesive has been 'killed' by sticking the tape down on a clean shiny surface such as glass, and then peeling it off. Do this a few times until it is only slightly tacky, otherwise there is a risk it will pull underlying paint away as it is removed after masking.

The tape is used to give sharp dividing lines between two colours, with scrap paper employed for the rest of the masking. I find that an old telephone directory is a good source of masking paper; I've been using one for ages now, and I've still got three-quarters of it left. Small gaps in the mask-

and *can* be sprayed over within a few minutes of the last coat. However, it is sensible before applying the top coats to let the final primer dry for a bit longer until it is hard. Very lengthy drying times are not a good idea, however, as the longer the model is left, the more chance there is that dust will settle on it. At the most, a couple of hours should be enough between coats. I normally aim to get the first coat of colour on within about half an hour of finishing priming.

Once you have achieved a reasonable finish on something simple like a wagon body, which is merely a case of overall spraying in a single colour, it will be a good idea to move on to a more advanced test piece, and for this a moulded plastic loco kit body or assembled plastic loco kit will be ideal. Pick one that calls for a two-colour livery (ie, not an all-black loco), so that you can try your hand at masking and other second-colour finishing techniques. Clean, prime and spray this test-piece carefully, and aim to get the best possible finish, as you may want to use this model for lining practice later.

The Desired Finish

What the 'best possible' paint finish might be is not always obvious; it depends largely on what you want to do with the model after the paint has been applied. If you are applying waterslide transfers, for instance, then you need a smooth, glossy surface on which the transfers will stick well. On the other hand, if you are intending to line out with a bowpen, then a matt or semi-matt surface will be better, as for reasons explained in the next chapter, pen lining does not work well on gloss surfaces. What is needed in all cases is a smooth finish that is thin enough not to obscure detail, does not have dust particles in it or untoward lumps and bumps under it, and which is adhering firmly to the model.

Masking

As well as getting paint where we do want it, it is often necessary to keep it away from certain parts of the model. This technique is known as 'masking', and is usually accomplished with ad-

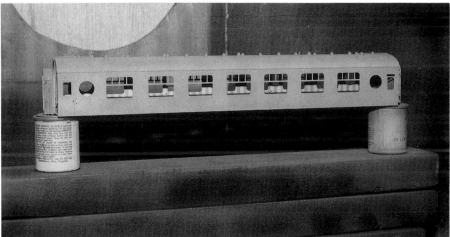

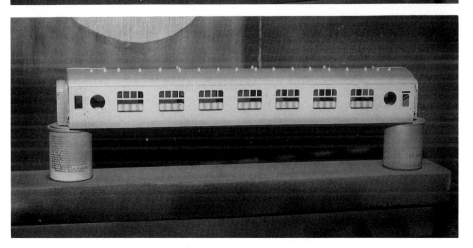

This is the LMS coach to be painted in crimson and cream. Top : The coach is cleaned and shot blasted. Middle : A coat of grey primer has been applied. Above : Two thin coats of BR Cream, from the Cherry Paints range, is applied.

hesive tape, paper and liquid masking solution. Masking is most often required when a second or subsequent colour is being applied over an initial coat of livery colour, although occasionally its purpose may be to keep some areas in bare primer so that a relatively translucent colour can be applied without the base colour showing through.

There are various types of masking tape, but for the delicate paintwork of our models we do not want anything too coarse. The masking tape I prefer is 'Cellux' low-tack, imported from Switzerland, which I find easy to use. An alternative is 'Frisk Film', available from many graphics or drawing office

ing which are awkward to cover with tape or paper should be sealed up with a liquid masking medium, such as Humbrol 'Maskol', a latex solution that can be brushed on. I know that some modellers don't get on too well with this stuff, but I have found that, provided it is dry before being painted over, and so long as it is removed from the model within a couple of days, then it shouldn't cause any problems.

Removing Masking

It is best to remove any masking as soon as the subsequent coat of paint has been sprayed, even while this is still wet. This will prevent the paint drying in a hard, crusty 'edge' where it has perhaps built up slightly against the masking tape. Peel the masking off with extreme care, and the paint will flatten out so that the dividing line is smooth. This spray, mask, spray, peel sequence is used for every subsequent colour sprayed on after the base colour. Some thought is needed to ensure that the colours go on in the right order to permit this to be done. After removing masking, check thoroughly to make sure that no base colour has been lifted by the masking. Sometimes, small fragments of paint do come away, but can usually be touched-in by brush without showing. However, anything much bigger than about 1mm. square will call for rubbing down and respraying, so go carefully.

Brush-Painting Secondary Colours

Masking can be avoided in the smaller scales - 4mm. and below - where it is possible to brush paint some or all of the secondary colours after the main colour has dried, although care must obviously be taken to avoid brush marks. This calls for good quality brushes, and paint thinned to just the right degree so that it will flow from the brush and onto the model without sticking to or dragging the surface of the underlying paint. This base coat needs to be absolutely dry, so if brush-painting of secondary colours is contemplated, allow the initial spray coat an extra twenty four

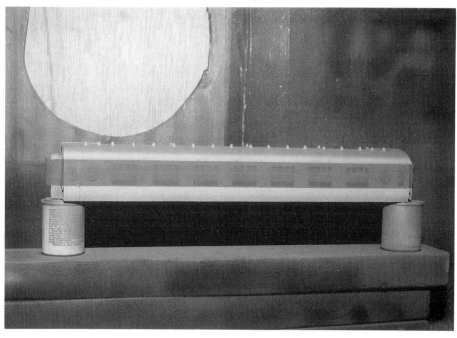

hours' drying time.

The Examples

I could go on talking in general terms about painting models, but it would seem much more worthwhile to look at some actual 'case histories'. As examples, I have chosen several models to illustrate some or all of the stages involved in applying a variety of liveries. These examples centre around a 7mm. scale Midland Railway Johnson 0-6-0 in the full glory of the Crimson Lake livery, as running about 1900.

This model was built by my friend Barry Fitch, who helped me out on the design of my NER transfer artwork. One good turn, as they say, deserves another - in this case, a coat of crimson paint.

The loco was built from a Jidenco Models (now Shedmaster) etched brass kit, and as can be seen from the photographs, is not *quite* complete. This is because Barry was good enough to let me have the loco to paint rather sooner than he would normally have liked, so that I was able to meet the

Top : It is masked off with the Cellux masking tape. Above : Spray with Cherry Paints BR Crimson and remove the masking whilst still wet. This illustration demonstrates just how easy it is to get it wrong and only mask off where you *think* the correct position is.

production schedule for this book. Fortunately, the items that he had been unable to fit, such as the tender brake gear and sanding pipes, could readily be installed once the paintwork was complete.

In addition to the MR 0-6-0, a number of other models were painted during the time that this book was in preparation. Although I have not shown each of these in full detail, I have used them from time to time to illustrate specific points, while most appear, in finished condition, in the colour section.

Most of the locos are in 7mm. scale, which made it easier to photograph things without tools or my hands obscuring too much. The coaches are to both 4 and 7mm. scales, depending on the particular lining technique being illustrated. The paints used are drawn from the ranges already described, and, with the exception of the Floquil used for an NER 4-4-0, are all readily available.

These examples have been chosen to give a representative selection of liveries and painting styles, as found on British railways in the steam age. Obviously, I cannot illustrate all the myriad colour schemes that have been applied to locos and rolling stock in this country, let alone those carried by foreign prototypes. However, the examples chosen call for the use of a range of techniques that could be equally well applied to other livery schemes.

Having discussed the painting process in only the most general way, it would now seem a good idea to look at the various types of livery and describe in detail how they are applied. Different types of livery call for different painting approaches and different combinations of techniques. The selection of examples I have chosen range from the simplest to the most complex of livery styles for both locos and coaches. In this chapter, I shall only be concerning myself with getting the paint onto these models; the lining comes in Chapter 7.

Lined Black Livery

LNER lined black in my case, but you could equally well read any other single lined livery, as the approach and method of application would be exactly the same. Of all the liveries applied to locomotives, this has to be the most straightforward after plain unlined black. As such, it makes a good starting point for those new to loco painting. Ordinary grey primer is a suitable basis, and I chose Cherry black eggshell as my preferred paint. A tip here regarding black locos; it is well worth masking off the buffer beams as described above with Maskol before the black is sprayed on, as the red paint used for these could take three or even four coats to cover the black, whereas two should suffice over grey primer. An alternative approach is to undercoat the bufferbeams in white applied over the black.

Normally, I would expect two coats of the eggshell black to do the job, with the second applied within the hour. The model would then be left overnight for the paint to harden, any bufferbeam masking having been removed as soon as practicable after the second coat. A thorough inspection in the morning will reveal any areas not covered properly, and if necessary, a third coat of black may be required. Don't forget to re-mask the bufferbeams! If all is well, then these should be finished off now. I usually use Humbrol Matt Red No. 60 or Gloss Red No. 19, depending on the finish required. It's an awful lot of trouble to mask off the rest of the engine just to spray these relatively small areas, so I usually brush paint. This would bring the model up to the lining stage, about which more in the next chapter.

Lined Green Livery

To be specific, NER lined green. In choosing this particular paint scheme, my own favourite, I might just as well have picked any loco painted in more than one main colour. The technique would be the same, whether the livery was GWR Brunswick or Highland Bronze. Once the main body colour -

Lined black livery on a NU Cast K2 Kit. If done properly, this livery can be one of the most realistic to produce. As can be seen, a lot of work was put in reducing the cast boiler bands.

NER green, in this instance - has been applied in the required number of coats, it must be allowed to harden thoroughly, for at least twenty-four hours after the final coat. Only then can it be masked up for the black areas of the footplate and smokebox to be sprayed.

I have painted many model locos in this livery, among them the NER 4-4-0 illustrated on the front cover. This model was built for a customer who had had previous locos finished with Floquil, so that was what I chose here. Floquil dries fairly matt, sometimes making for difficulties when it comes to applying transfers, which often do not stick well to a matt surface. It may on occasion be necessary to spray on a coat of gloss varnish before applying transfers, especially waterslide transfers. Unfortunately, this particular lo-

comotive did not lend itself to being built in sub-assemblies, which made the job of painting and, especially, lining it quite a bit harder.

Lined Madder Lake Livery

Much of what applied to the NER lined green livery applies equally to the North Staffs lined madder lake livery. The actual 'Madder Lake' is from the Cherry range, and hence gives a gloss finish rather than my preferred matt. I have to admit being quite taken with the colour, which is a deeper, browner shade than Midland Crimson Lake. I hope the photograph on the back cover brings out the richness of the result. This livery was chosen partly to illustrate the difficulties sometimes encountered when there is very little prototype information available. More on this aspect later.

I am fortunate that Ray Ward, the builder of the 7mm scale NSR 2-4-0T illustrated, was thoughtful enough to make the boiler assembly detachable, rendering the painting and lining of this model a great deal easier. The various operations and stages all still have to be carried out, but the masking and lining of separate components is a lot more straightforward than hav-

ing to negotiate things like the leading springs, which would get in the way. Ray had also omitted pipework and other parts which needed to be left polished, which cuts out some tricky masking and keeps pipes and so on out of the way of the lining at the later stages of the paint job. These components were fitted when all the paintwork was completed.

Crimson Lake coach livery

I have chosen this common pre-group painting style mostly to illustrate how reasonably complicated *lining* is applied. The paint application stages are more or less the same as for the other examples. However, as suggested back in Chapter 3, the primer used this time would be the red oxide type, chosen to make the coverage of the top coat that much easier. With

Madder Lake livery - see back cover for the colour version. About as far removed from the lined black livery as you can get!

any panelled coach, it is important to make sure that the paint gets in to the corners where the beading meets the side; if the paint has been mixed a little too thin, this is where it will show up. It is feasible of course to paint these types of coach side before assembly, always a useful possibility with a plastic coach kit. With reasonable care in keeping adhesive off the surfaces, glued assembly of a pre-painted plastic kit will not affect the finish in the way that the use of a hot soldering iron undoubtedly would on a painted brass model.

One problem with coaches is that they have a lot of windows - which need to be transparent, not painted over! It is thus obviously easier to paint the coach sides *before* installing the glazing. This is another job where painting the sides before assembling the coach makes life easier. I absolutely hate glazing coaches, particularly those with individual compartments. I've developed a method for glazing metal coaches, which, although strictly outside the scope of this book, I pass on because I know that others have the same dread of fitting plastic glazing and getting it to stick to brass. I happened on it by sheer chance, but it does seem to work.

Basically, it goes like this:- I cut all the 'Plastiglaze' glazing for both sides of the coach to the correct sizes. I then put a thin film of Bostick All Purpose Adhesive around each window aperture. This process is repeated for the second side, and by the time that is finished, the glue on the first side will have dried clear. If it has not, it should be left until it does. The glazing can then be placed in position, the Bostik remaining very slightly tacky at this stage. When happy with the position

of the glazing, Mek-Pak is run round the edge of each piece of glazing, taking care to keep it off the visible portion, and left to dry. Essentially, what happens is that the Bostik sticks to the metal coach side, and the Mek-Pak sticks the plastic glazing to the Bostik.

Two colour coach liveries

Although my specific concern was with BR crimson and cream, the methods described could be used for any other two colour coach livery, such as the GWR's chocolate and cream, the LNWR 'Plum and Spilt Milk', or the basically similar LSWR and L&Y liveries. The shades of crimson and cream used by BR seem to have caused a bit of controversy recently, with some debate about how they are best reproduced on a model. It seems difficult to

pin down the specific shade used by BR, so once again I chose colours which suited my eye; let the doubters prove me wrong! The particular colours I use are from the Cherry Paints range, although Railmatch also list them in their collection.

The usual way of applying any two colour livery like this is to spray the lighter colour first, as the darker colour will always cover the lighter better than vice-versa. The problem with the crimson and cream livery is that the crimson really needs to have a red oxide primer, whereas cream usually won't cover this too well. A compromise is needed, and here I use the grey primer, and spray a test piece at the same time. I can then use the test piece with the crimson to see if it will cover. If not, it is easy enough to spray a thin coat of Humbrol bauxite on to

Midland Railway enthusiasts will immediately spot that the livery is wrong for the coach in this condition. However, I painted this about twenty years ago when I didn't know any better. A good case for checking the model against photographs if they are available, which I have to say were not at the time.

the coach after masking off the initial coat of cream, applied first. There will then be no problem with the crimson covering properly.

Allow at least twenty four hours for the first colour - in this case, the cream - to dry before masking off, as the paint needs to be really hard. Masking is with tape, aiming to get a nice sharp line to divide the colours. Coach masking has a few more pitfalls than masking a locomotive, as there is a long line where the tape needs to be stuck down firmly and straight, and if your cleaning and priming have not been done properly this will find you out. Again, it is important to remove the tape while the second colour is still wet to avoid the paint build up. It is even more important here, as the division of the colours has to be lined over, and a ridge or step in the paint will make this very difficult.

If you are feeling really brave, then, after another twenty four hours, the whole of the coach sides should be masked, and the ends sprayed, possibly followed by the roof. However, many modellers prefer to brush paint the roof to give this some texture, particularly on vehicles with a canvas roof covering. This needs to be done with a matt paint, as shiny coach roofs just don't look right unless your layout runs in the rain. To avoid finger marks on the finish - a problem with many matt paints - a thin coat of matt varnish over the roof is worthwhile. After a few hours to let this dry, and after lining and transfers are in place, I give the sides and ends a coat of gloss varnish

to finally seal everything. This is drifted on at a fairly high pressure so that the effect is not too glossy. More of this later.

While all this is going on with the coach body, I get the interior, underframes and bogies ready. There is nothing really remarkable here, save that interiors are all brush painted, with the underframe and bogies being sprayed dull black. The whole assembly was then given a coat of satin varnish before final assembly.

Lined Teak livery

Up until a few years ago, teak livery seemed to be a complete mystery to many modellers but is now reckoned fairly easy to apply. The most popular methods all seem to have a background colour over which is laid a thin top coat giving the effect of the varnished teak. I first came across this a few years ago from a fellow club member, but similar methods are recommended by both Precision and Cherry.

Again, it is much easier to paint and line the coach sides before assembly. Personally, I do prefer to paint the coach in stages as it is being built, but I have at least one friend (who builds a lot of coaches) who always finishes the sides of plastic coaches before starting to build anything. The first step in producing a teak finish is to give the coach sides a coat of primer, followed by a base colour undercoat. This dictates the finished effect, giving either a lighter or darker teak. For this base coat I use either Humbrol No. 62 for the lighter effect, or No. 63

for the darker. This can be brushed or sprayed on, as we are not looking for a super smooth finish.

When this is completely dry, a thin coat of Humbrol red oxide is brushed over the top, so that it doesn't cover completely. Some experimenting on a test piece will soon give you the idea. I try and get a fifty - fifty mix of paint and thinners on a small palette and then brush it on. The brush strokes must run in the same direction as the grain, as they are what gives the grained effect. Remember that on GNR and LNER coaches, the grain of the teak runs vertically above the waist line and horizontally below. As all the colours used so far have been matt, the teak effect will not look very prepossessing until a coat of varnish is applied. But as the side needs to be lined before varnishing, this cannot be done until the final stages of the paint job.

Ready for the Lining

Thus far, this book has concerned itself almost entirely with the business of getting paint onto the model in as controlled and effective a manner as possible. Although in many cases this will be the end of the matter, most steam era liveries call for some degree of lining. This is seen by many as the hardest part of the job. Lining is made a great deal easier though if it is being applied to the sort of smooth, even paint finish that the techniques described should enable you to achieve.

GNR/LNER Teak livery. Graining is vertical on the upper panels and horizontal on the lower ones.

Chapter Seven
LINING

The NER 290 Class as shown earlier.

The lining of models causes as much heartache and soul-searching as anything else in the hobby. It is all too easy to turn even the best-built model into one of the worst-looking, simply by applying uneven, second-rate lining. Fortunately, the reverse is also true, and a really good lining and finishing job will often make a rather poorly built model look a good deal better than it really is. The important thing is to approach the job in the right frame of mind, which means as relaxed as possible. This is helped by using good quality tools for the job, and adopting techniques that allow you to correct mistakes.

Tools for Lining

I think it obvious that, to stand any chance of making a decent job of lining, a good instrument for drawing the lines is vital. As yet, I have found nothing better than the draughtsmans' bowpen. This is in spite of all the gadgets that come on to the market from time to time, often amid claims that they are the answer to all lining problems. I'm sorry to say that, having tried them all, so far I haven't found this to be true, and I always end up back with my bowpen.

The best of these specialised devices is undoubtedly Bob Moore's 'lining pen', which does work quite nicely in much the same way as a Rotring tube-type drawing pen. The snag is that, even with the 'fine' head, it still produces a

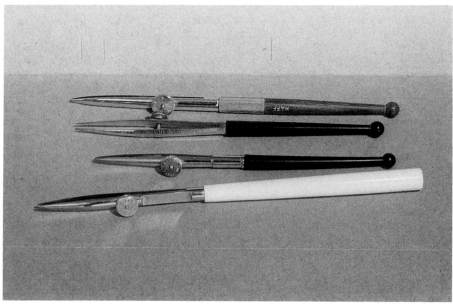

A selection of bow pens - HAFF, KERN and a couple not identified. Chosen for the length of the blades all will draw reasonably fine lines.

line which is two or three times the width that I can achieve with a bowpen. This is not a problem in the larger scales (for which it was developed), but those working to 4mm. or smaller will struggle to get acceptable results. To obtain the fine lines needed in 4mm - and for some 7mm liveries as well - with this pen, it is necessary to overlay lines so that each succeeding line covers part of the one that went before it. With a bit of thought and care, this method *can* give good results, with the lines obtained at least being of constant width. The biggest

snag is that the painted lines will tend to build up on the surface, giving a rather thick and clumsy look. This can be a real problem in the smaller scales, although the technique has been used with success even in 2mm.

Bowpens

Unfortunately, bowpens are becoming rather scarce as their traditional role in drawing offices has been taken over by the Rotring tube-and-needle pens and now by computer plotters. Rotring type tube pens do have a use as a lining instrument, as we shall see

42

Use an instrument for drawing straight lines.

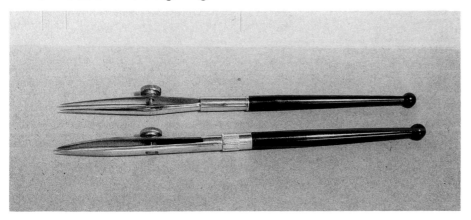

The Kern (top) and Ecobra.

later in this chapter, but it is the traditional bowpen we really want. Good drawing office suppliers and graphics/art shops should be able to get you one even if they no longer keep them in stock.

What you are looking for is an instrument similar to those shown in the photograph, with reasonably long, thin blades tapering down to a fairly sharp point. The inside faces of the blades must be absolutely flat and smooth otherwise paint will not flow freely from them. The tips of the blades should meet accurately, and should be easy to adjust, with the knurled nut running on a fine screw thread. Throughout my time as a professional modelmaker, I have been using pens made by Kern in Switzerland, but much to my dismay they ceased manufacture a year or two ago. This left me quite worried until, a little while later, a friend (thanks Paul) showed me a way of sharpening pens, which meant I could improve lesser pens to somewhere near the standard of the Kern.

More recently, I have come across an alternative to the Kern that seems as good. This is the Ecobra bowpen, made in Germany. They are not cheap, and although they differ in some respects from the Kern design, they draw lines that are just as fine which, at the end of the day, is what matters. Suppliers of these pens are listed in the sources index at the end of the book.

Finding a good bowpen is not easy, but possible sources are junk or antique shops, which may have old sets of drawing instruments for sale, often quite cheaply. Some of these old Victorian pens can be superb, with really fine steel blades and an ivory handle. They can be cleaned, sharpened and rehabilitated, and can give really fine results. A couple of years ago, whilst I was demonstrating at Scaleforum, a gentleman showed me a drawing set, including bowpens, bought from a junkshop for a fiver. I offered to double his money on the spot, but I must have seemed too keen, as he wouldn't sell! Still, it shows that these things are around if you look hard enough.

Sharpening Bowpens

What we are looking for in a bowpen are tips that are as fine as possible, but not sharp, as we don't want to score the paint. These tips do wear and become blunt, which will result in thicker lines, but we can restore matters by sharpening the blades. Examine the tips of the pen under a magnifying glass, and see what sort of shape they are in. We want them to be fine, but rounded on all the edges. To thin them down, they can be filed with a fine Swiss file and finished off with emery paper. Work on the outside of the blades if you can, as it's important to make sure they still meet accurately at the inside of the tips. Aim to get a very smooth, clean finish, especially on

the insides where the paint will flow. Keep trying the pen on a painted test piece until you have got it right.

Paints for Lining

To go with our bowpen, we need a suitable lining medium. I use enamels more or less exclusively, but other modellers use acrylics or other water-based paints like designers colour (gouache). This enables them to wash away mistakes made when lining on an enamel surface with water, which obviously won't affect the underlying enamel. I have to say that I've tried acrylics, but they just don't seem to suit me. As enamels do, then that's a good enough reason to stick with them.

The enamel that I use for lining is, almost exclusively, Humbrol. Most of the colours are the fast-drying matt type, as this means the model can be handled only a short time after the lines have been drawn, reducing the risk of smudging and spoiling all that hard work. I also find it important to use fresh paint for lining, so if you are only going to line one or two models a year, it is worth paying out the extra 65p or so to have a fresh tin for this work, especially when you consider the money and the hours of work put into the construction of the model. If well stirred, the consistency of fresh Humbrol will be exactly right for lining. I have often heard the thinning of enamel advocated when lining with a bowpen - this is quite wrong in my experience; it does not. All that thin paint gives you is a wider line than necessary. I suspect that those modellers who suggest thinning are trying to use old paint, where much of the carrier has evaporated. On the other hand, I occasionally come across the odd tin of new Humbrol that has too much carrier, and is thus too thin to start with. In this case, it is best to leave the lid off overnight (keep it out of the dust, though) to allow excess carrier to evaporate.

Other Lining Tools

As well as the bowpen, there are some other implements needed to line models. The first, and most obvious, is a rule or selection of rules, the longest of which will enable you to draw the maximum length of line you need in one go. I have three, all plastic, the longest an ordinary twelve inch rule, the other two being seven inches and

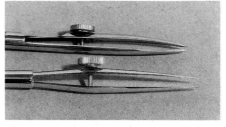

If you are looking to obtain a suitable bow pen, this is what to look for. Fairly long blades tapering down to points which, although not sharp enough to cut, are fairly well honed.

five inches respectively, made by suitable surgery on other twelve inch rules. I prefer the plastic ones as they are far less likely to mark the surface of the model than steel. I will use whatever size best suits the model I'm lining - obviously, the larger the ruler, the more difficult it is to handle.

For drawing curves, a set of 'French', or Draughtsmans' curves is useful, plus some draughtsmans' templates for circles and ellipses. The French curves include parabolic curves and transitions, but are hard to get in really small sizes suited to lining locos in 4mm scale or smaller. The other templates do go down to very small sizes. If there is no suitable ready-made template, I make my own from 20thou. Plastikard, which can be cut and filed to shape. Circles of any desired radius can be cut out of this with a very sharp pair of dividers. Also useful for drawing larger circular lines and for lining

'Draughtsmans' curves. Basically a template for drawing around, they can also be used for estimating radii when cutting plastic card templates.

wheel rims is a small pair of compasses with bowpen attachment. These were often included in the older sets of drawing instruments already described.

Brushes for Lining

For touching in the rounded corners of panels, we need fine good quality

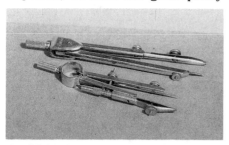

Useful for drawing curves and circles.

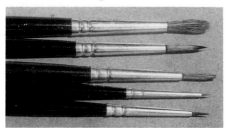

A selection of Windsor and Newton brushes, the five shown fulfil about 95% of the work I do.

paintbrushes. This means sable, and I use either Windsor & Newton series 12 in a 000 size or, if I can get them, the series 29 spotting sables, which go down to a 00000.

Lining Practice

With a good bowpen and the right paint, lining is a task which becomes a good deal more straightforward. However, that's not to say that just by having a good pen and some new Humbrol you will become a lining 'ace' overnight. Practice is the only way to acquire the skill that will enable you to draw fine, consistent-width lines on all parts of your model. This consistency of line width is very important; nothing spoils the job more than lining which wanders about from hair-thin to heavy. It is better to establish a width of line which you can be sure of drawing all the time, rather than going for a super-fine line if you can't keep it up.

Remember also that many lining schemes call for curved corners, which will have to be put in with your small brush. These curves need to be the same width as the straight lines, so the brush may limit the possible line width.

Initially, it will be best to practice on the flat rather than on an actual

20 thou Plastic Card test piece, and a small template cut from the same material. This piece was actually for lining under the cab roof on the NSR 2-4-0T. The cut out is to clear the tail from the safety valves.

model. My recommendation is to start by spraying up a piece of Plastikard of about A5 size. Once the paint is really dry and hard, this will give the same sort of surface as a painted model. Lining on the flat like this is always good practice, as indeed most of the lining on models will be applied to flat sur-

faces. The only real exceptions are boiler bands, but it is often best to draw these on the flat and transfer them to the model afterwards; the making of such transfers is covered in the next section. Once you are happy that you have the hang of lining 'flat', you may like to have a go on your practice plastic loco body, which I suggested painting as a test piece in the last chapter.

Assuming that this is painted in an appropriate colour - and I for one can see no point whatsoever in painting models in silly or fictitious liveries, even as practice pieces - it is a good idea to attempt a full lining job on it. Hopefully, you will have achieved a good paint surface, and once this is thoroughly dry and hard, you can start to apply lining, once again following correct prototype practice for colour and style. If you come across some particularly difficult lining, which you feel you may be unable to apply successfully, then you have to decide whether it can be left off, or whether it must be attempted. There is a good case for leaving off some sorts of lining, but if you leave out too much you run the risk that the model just won't look right. Lining a loco body as practice will also suggest which areas you find easy to apply direct, and which might be best made as transfers.

Making Lining Transfers

My preference is to put as much lining as possible straight onto the model, completing the rest as necessary with transfers. With lined boiler bands, transfers are more or less essential, although I *have* seen models with the bands lined 'in situ'. I don't like using too many transfers, though, as there is the chance that they may not stick properly, and hence will tend to come off with handling. On the other hand, for some liveries, particularly very complex ones, it may be better to draw *all* the lining onto transfer sheet for later application, as it will be easier to correct mistakes and, should the worst

happen, you can always start again without affecting the model or its paintwork.

Although transfers are usually the last parts of the lining to be applied, they need to be made well in advance to allow the paint to dry properly. Preparing your own 'in house' trans-

Lining on the splasher tops. Similar to boiler band lining using a transfer. The required shape and design is drawn onto the painted sheet, cut out and slid into place.

Drawing boiler band lining.

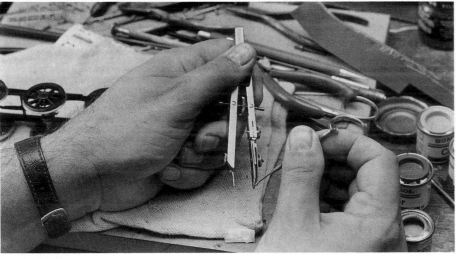

Loading the pens.

Testing the flow.

fers is extremely easy, being no harder than lining on that test piece of Plastikard. Waterslide transfer paper (see sources index) is simply substituted for the Plastikard, and is painted and lined in exactly the same way. As the name implies, this type of transfer film is released from the carrier paper by soaking in water, which also acts as a lubricant to enable the transfer to be slid into place. As the water is removed by blotting or by evaporation, the transfer film, complete with painted lining, sticks to the surface of the model, shrinking very slightly in the process. Waterslide transfers, whether home-made or commercial, do not stick well to matt paint finishes, which have a rather granular surface. If this is a problem they should then be applied over gloss or varnish (see later) and matted down later as required.

Boilerband Transfers

These hand-lined transfers are the best way to apply boilerbands. The trick is to cut out the lining complete with backing paper, lay this around the boiler, then wet the whole thing. After a few moments, the backing paper will separate from the carrier film. When this happens, the backing can be eased away, leaving the film in place ready for final adjustment. The thick-ness of the film is only a couple of thou., but this is about right to represent the scale thickness of a boiler band, which on the prototype is only made of thin steel strip. In fact, even 2thou. is too much in 4mm scale, but OK in 7mm. If you don't fancy drawing your own boiler bands, ready-printed waterslide bands are available from Kemco, although these aren't as fine as can be ruled by hand. It is a pity that so many kit locos have etched or cast-on boiler bands that are far too thick, even before lining is applied. These need thinning down even if lining isn't to be applied.

Lining with the Bowpen

We begin by loading the pen. For this, I use a very small screwdriver or cocktail stick, and let a small drop of paint run into the tips of the pen blades, which have been closed down so that there is a gap of about 1mm. Capillary action will draw the paint down to the ends of the blades, so that it remains there as the blades are adjusted down to give the required line width, and is ready to flow out as the pen is drawn across the painted surface. A few practice strokes should always be made before the pen is applied to the model, and this I usually do on the top of my plastic rule, which has a surface not unlike the painted model. Once I am happy that the paint is flowing properly and that the pen is drawing the right width of line, I can start lining.

As can be seen from the photographs, I hold the pen at an angle of about 45 degree to the horizontal, and draw it steadily along the face of the rule. The only way to assess the amount of pressure to apply is by practising, which is why that sheet of painted Plastikard is so useful. Too much pressure, and the tips of the pen blades will cut into the paint surface; too little, and the line will not be continuous, as the paint flow will keep stopping and starting. Try to avoid breathing in mid-line, too. Take a deep breath before you start, and relax as far as you can. Tension does not help, and holding the pen too rigidly can cause it to 'dig in'. Once you have got the knack, however, a good constant-width line will result every time.

If you have problems, first check that the paint thickness is right and that the pen is clean and properly set. Also make sure that no grease or dirt has got onto the painted surface over which you are trying to line. Sometimes, however, for no apparent reason, the paint just won't flow properly, stopping in the middle of a line or refusing to start. Often, it's just a case of persevering, trying not to get tense, which never helps. If it just won't go right, it may well be best to leave it, and try again on a different occasion. I suspect that there are other factors, such as atmospheric conditions and tiredness (whether or not induced by too much Boddingtons the night before), which affect the delicate lining process without our being aware of them.

Lining on Glossy Surfaces

We noted in the chapter on spraying that, if we need to line a loco, we should avoid if possible ending up with a glossy finish to the main paint job. This is because, when the pen is drawn across the paint surface, something is needed to break the surface tension of the lining colour and allow it to flow. The lining colour, being matt paint, has a relatively high level of surface tension which tends to hold it between the pen blades. A matt surface to the underlying paint, being considerably rougher than gloss, is better at breaking this tension, and 'pulls' the paint nicely from the pen.

One of the reasons for using the top of my plastic rule for trying the pen before lining is to get the paint flowing in the same way, as I find that the indentations and printing on the rule are quite good at getting the paint moving. Once the it is flowing freely from the pen, start lining on the loco at once. If you *must* line over gloss paint, you may find it helpful to use gloss paint in the pen, as this has a lower surface tension than the matt, and will hence flow more readily on a smooth surface. Beware that you don't smudge the end result, though, as it takes a lot longer to dry.

Lining Technique

As many of the straight lines as pos-

Mixing the paint. Rices workshop could only summon up a humble cock-tail stick for this exercise.

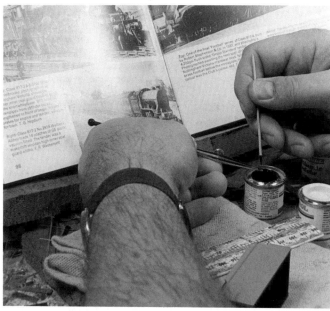

The corners of each panel should be measured and a faint pencil dot marked. The black lines can then be drawn into place followed by the white lines. Corners are touched in with a brush.

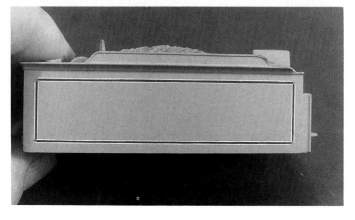

sible are put in first using the various rules, followed by the major curved lines on splasher fronts or tender copings. These will call for templates - the ready-made draughtsman's type if you're lucky, but (more than likely) home-made. You will often need two such templates, for the inner and outer radii of double lining respectively. Use the ready made draughtsman's template to work out the appropriate radii, and cut out the required circles from 20thou. Plastikard. To hold the template in position while it is being used, I either keep it pressed down with the tip of a craft knife held in my free hand, or retain it with a tiny dab of Blu-Tack. Take care when removing Blu-Tack from the painted surface; if it doesn't want to come off easily, *roll* another small piece of Blu-Tack across the stubborn bit, which should peel off cleanly.

Making Lining Templates

I use my sharp dividers for this, keeping the cutting tip in good condition with fine wet-and-dry paper. Draw the required radius on the Plastikard, making a series of passes until the cut is deep enough to allow the resulting circle to be pressed out of the sheet of Plastikard. The edge should be cleaned and smoothed, with the undercut resulting from the dividers action being

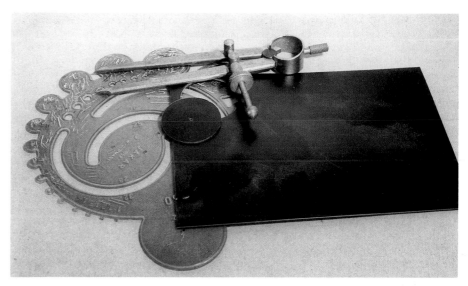

Making a template for lining. Use sharpened dividers to cut the radius needed.

sight to *see* those, let alone draw them. On a good day, with everything going right, I find that I can draw a 0.2mm line consistently. I *can* get finer than that, but not over a whole model.

For this LNER livery, as for the virtually identical LMS version, the lining colour called for is vermilion, and for this I used Humbrol No. 54 'Matt Scarlet'. I also generally use this colour for bufferbeams. The single straight lines were put in, followed by the curves. For the front splashers, I

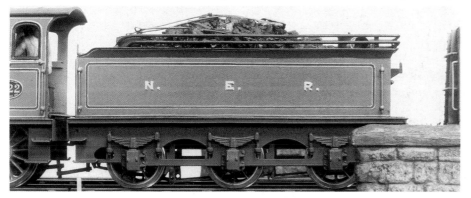

How the tender side should look.

carefully preserved. This will prevent paint running back under the template when it is held down on the surface of the model and lined around. Don't throw away these templates when you've used them - they may well come in useful for some future model.

Lining - Some Specific Examples

LNER lined black livery:This livery has a single fine red line bordering the black panels. When I say fine, I mean fine, as such a line on the prototype would have been only about a quarter or three eighths of an inch wide. That's around 0.0125mm. at 4mm. scale, and even at 7mm/ft, as on the N2 illustrated in the clour section, a mere 0.22mm. wide. So we need to draw some pretty fine lines even in this larger scale, and this for lining that is quite heavy compared with some. One-eighth lines were common on pre-grouping prototypes, and in our model scales you would need pretty good eye-

needed several templates, for where the splashers meet the sandboxes there is a double line, one each side of the beading, while the same sort of

Using the same compass and pen to line wheel tyres.

thing occurs with the bottom of the main splasher and the coupling rod splasher. These templates were a bit tricky to make, as they had to fit in place on the splasher front but avoid the coupling rod splasher.

NER lined green livery:in this case, as with most locos having liveries with a central black line between other colours, I prefer to get these black lines in place first. I start by marking the locations of the corners of the main panels of lining on the tender, using a soft pencil and placing the marks so that the black lining will cover them. Next, the straight lines forming the sides of the panel are drawn. These should be 0.58mm wide in 7mm. scale. It is not possible to produce a steady line of that width with one pass of the pen, so two or even three passes, each overlapping slightly, are needed. Succeeding passes should be made quickly, so that all the paint is still wet and can blend into a single smooth line. The corners are then laid in with the 000 paintbrush.

The tender is then put aside for the black lines to harden, and the loco body tackled. While the cabside panels can be applied in the same way as the tender sides, a different approach is needed with the splashers, which are not only lined both sides of the bead-

Finished lining on the tyres.

Using the compass and pen attachment for lining the wheel splashers. A piece of softwood held in place with a rubber band.

Apart from the lining on the splashers already shown, and the cab sides, the rest were applied with transfers, such as the boiler bands and those on the cab front.

ing, but panelled out as well. This creates something a problem, and careful planning is needed to get this complex lining right. In this case, I feel that the Plastikard templates already described for the N2 are not the best approach. Instead, I opted to use the compass bowpen.

Using the compass pen obviously calls for something to stick the compass point into, and my usual solution is a block of softwood cut to fit inside the loco body. This needs to stick out far enough below the running plate to cater for the centre of the arc of the splasher. An alternative is to fix a suitable wooden block below the running

plate, either using the body fixing holes and mounting screws or clamping it in place with strong rubber bands, as illustrated on the MR 0-6-0 in the photo. Once the pivot-point of the compass is established for each set of circular curves, they can all be drawn accurately and concentrically. Don't move the wooden block between lining colours, as you'll lose this accuracy. On the NER 4-4-0, this technique allowed me to get both the black central line and the twin white borders in exactly the right place.

Most of the rest of the lining on this 4-4-0, the application of the fine white

lines bordering on either side of the wide black ones, was accomplished in the same way as the simple scheme on the N2. The difference is that there's just a lot more of it to apply! However, due to the fact that this model was built as a single unit, there were a few places where I found that I just couldn't get the pen in to draw the lining. The splasher tops and cab front were a case in point; the NER treated these as, effectively, a single panel, with a black border edged with a single white line starting from where the splasher met the footplate at the front, going along the entire splasher top, up the front edge of the cab, across under the cab roof and back down the same way on the other side.

Although it would have been possible to draw the section along the top of the splashers directly, in the interests of consistency I decided to make all this lining as a transfer. The lining could thus be drawn in the flat onto the transfer paper in one go, giving nice consistent lines, even though it then had to be cut into manageable sections for application. As well as the black and white panels and borders on the green, this NER loco is typical of pre-grouping schemes in having the black framing lined with a single vermilion line, as in the simple livery of the N2. These lines were applied by pen as for the N2, using templates cut and filed to shape from Plastikard to line around the cut-outs in the tender frames. The same technique was used to line out the tender underframe of the MR 0-6-0 illustrated.

NSR Madder Lake: the basic lining technique used for this livery was much as for the NER lined green, although in this case there were a few additional snags. For a start, precise prototype information on this NSR lining scheme proved hard to come by, as is often the case with the more obscure pre-grouping liveries. My main source was a book, 'North Staffordshire Locos', which has some livery notes. These called for a cream line, an inch wide, six inches in from the edges of the panels lined, in this case the tank and bunker sides and the bunker rear. This was straightforward enough in 7mm. scale, and I marked out the panel corners with my soft pencil as already described for the 4-4-0. But the specification also called for a 'thin vermilion line' either side of this wide cream line. How thin is thin? As fine as I could manage, I decided. I soon found, however, that drawing a fine vermilion line onto Madder Lake had a snag; I couldn't see it! I went through four different paint shades and types before finding Humbrol Gloss Red No.19 which stood out sufficiently to register.

Apart from the boiler bands and buffer beams, no specific mention is made in the book or the other sources I consulted about the rest of the NSR lining. So it was down to what I could learn from knowledgeable friends like

As well as black and white lining the LNER along with other companies used a single red line. It would often not show up on contemporary photos so we have to rely on other information to ensure accuracy.

fers for some types of coach lining for flush sided vehicles, as already described. When lining onto a coach side, I use a twelve inch rule, held in place by a small piece of Blu-Tack under the right hand end; the rule can then be controlled with the left hand, leaving the right to manage the pen. It is possible to secure both ends of the rule with Blu-Tack, although it is more of a fiddle to move it when required. I tend to do this on the longer coach sides, for it is useful to have a hand free to steady things when drawing very long lines.

The BR painting instructions for the famous 'blood and custard' cream-over-crimson are quite specific, and I followed them in painting the ex-LMS coach in this example. The roof was given as 'light grey', with the guttering or cornice black. The cream panel was to be 'the full height of the windows plus one inch above and below'. Above the cream would be a black line "edged in gold, the black to lie next to the cream". The black line was three quarters of an inch wide, and the gold three eighths. All other parts of the coach sides were to be 'crimson lake', and the ends black.

Applying this livery to an ex-LMS coach caused a few problems. The cream went on first, followed by the crimson and then the black ends and solebars and the grey roof. The requirement for one inch of cream to be left above and below the windows meant masking off to give a line of cream only one third of a millimetre wide at these locations. The answer was to make this cream portion a bit bigger than that, and to put the black and gold lining on top of part of it to get the remaining visible portion somewhere near right.

Ian Rathbone and the manufacturer of this 2-4-0T kit (Knotty Kits - the 'Knotty' being the affectionate nickname for the North Staffs, whose emblem was the 'Staffordshire Knot'). From all these sources, I learned that I needed to edge the various panels and the footplate angles (valences) in black and cream. The boiler bands were also cream, once again edged with the 'fine vermilion line'. My experience suggested that this vermilion line would also be used elsewhere on the loco, where the cream and Madder Lake met. The panel edges, for instance, would equate to 'half a boiler band', calling for the vermilion inside the cream. So I applied it in all these situations, and was gratified to be vindicated, when later shown a contemporary F. Moore's colour painting of an NSR tank loco in this livery, where it is clearly shown. The end result of my efforts is illustrated on the cover.

Fortunately, most of the more popular pre-group liveries are well documented, but there are many problems along the way and researching a livery for a model can sometimes take longer than actually applying it.

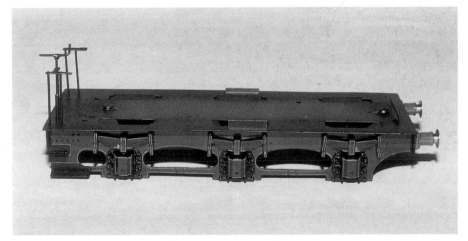

If it sticks out line it. This is the tender footplate frames and axleboxes from the Midland 0-6-0. Just how far some companies went with their lining is shown here.

COACH LIVERIES;
Crimson Lake,
Crimson-and-Cream,
Lined Teak

Coaches are generally lined out in much the same way as locomotives. I usually prefer to use the bowpen to line direct onto the painted coach side, although it is possible to make trans-

However, producing this lining isn't easy either, as the gold line should really end up only about 0.125mm wide. To achieve this, the first black line was put on at a bit less than 0.25mm, and as near to 0.75mm from the window edge as possible. This was followed by a gold line of the same width, being more or less the narrowest line it is possible to draw reliably.

This is how it should be done and what it should look like.

A second black line was then ruled overlapping both the first black and the gold line, narrowing the gold line and giving a black line of the correct 0.25mm width and, hopefully, leaving around 0.3mm of cream showing above and below the windows.

This coach was painted in Cherry paints, once again giving the typical glossy finish. This enabled me to wipe off any lining errors with a tissue slightly moistened with thinners without damaging the paint, as can be done when lining onto cellulose. This glossy finish would also have accepted waterslide lining transfers readily, had I decided to use this approach.

The panelled-out crimson lake livery typical of MR/LMS coaches calls for a different approach. The lining here is a central black line on the beading, which is edged with fine yellow lines. Although I would normally put these central black lines on first, in this case I reverse the order and line the yellow first, aiming to get the lines as close as possible to the outside edge of the beading, and not worrying too much about the inner edges. It doesn't really matter what happens in the middle of the beading, as the idea is to rule the black over the centre, leaving only a fine yellow edging showing.

The central black line can be ruled on, not necessarily with the bowpen and Humbrol, but with a Rotring tube-type draughtsman's pen and black draughting ink. These Rotring pens won't pass Humbrol-type paints with-

If there is a simple starting point on coach lining, this is it. All the beading is square cornered, so only straight lines need to be drawn.

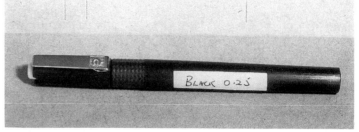

The Rotring drawing pen. This happens to be manufactured by Staedeler, but the principle is the same from any make. Ink is drawn down from the well through capillary action and into a fine nib. 0.25mm is about right for drawing the centre of beading on Midland 4mm coaches.

Pen held steady by using a rule.

out extensive thinning, at least not in the small nib sizes that we need for lining work, so they aren't much use to us generally. They are designed for use with special waterproof drawing inks, which are available in a wide range of colours; these work fine on paper, but are no good over paint as they are too transparent and just don't show up. The exception to this is the black, which is sufficiently dense and covers well, hence its use here. The pen used was the 025 (0.25mm wide line) size, with a white colour code band for the nib unit. Although the ink touch-dries very quickly, it takes a few days to really harden, and can be dissolved by meths. So, where this is being used for applying Methfix transfers, beware! The ink also doesn't flow too well onto a gloss surface, so it may pay to apply a semi-matt varnish before lining with a Rotring pen.

The usefulness of the Rotring and black ink is really confined to 4mm scale and below. In 7mm, the areas to be covered are too large, and there tends to be a lot of ink about, which takes much longer to dry than a fine line, and can easily run or smudge. The danger of meths from methfix transfers causing the ink to run is also more of a problem with large areas. If you do use a Rotring to line large areas, varnish over the ink as soon as it is properly dry, to protect it.

As you will see from the photographs, this panelled livery can come in two versions, with square or rounded corners. The square corner version is very easy to do once basic lining has been mastered, as the straight lines are simply ruled until they meet up at the corners. For the rounded variant, the corners must be put in freehand with the No.000 sable brush, as the radii are too small, even in 7mm scale, to be ruled with templates.

Our final example, the Gresley teak finish, also needs to be lined out. At first glance, this appears to be the easiest of the lot, being a single primrose yellow down the centre of the beadings. In fact, this isn't quite the case, as this quarter inch yellow line was flanked by two one sixteenth inch vermilion lines. At 4mm scale, these come out at about 0.02mm - less than

1 thou. - wide, which is impossible to reproduce. Here is a case where it's best to turn a blind eye, and leave off the vermilion altogether. The yellow lines need to be pretty fine anyway, and are ruled on direct with the pen and Humbrol No.81 Pale Yellow paint.

With the lining in place, the next stage in completing the paint job is to apply lettering or other insignia. This is usually done with transfers, as described in the next chapter. However, before moving on to this stage, it may be necessary to apply a coat of varnish. This has two purposes - to protect the lining, and to provide a suitable surface on which to lay transfers. As we have already noted, a different quality of surface is often needed at the various stages of the painting process.

Ink applied to some of the beading (top) and the finished article (below). With care it looks most affective.

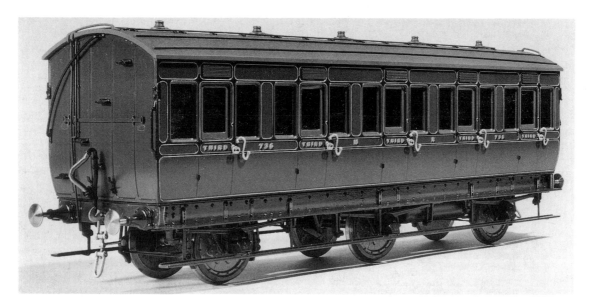

In some respects I find MR coach livery one of the most satisfying to do. It looks very untidy until all the lines are put in, and is quite time consuming to do. However, the finished article can be very pleasing. The method is as shown earlier, with the corners drawn in with a 000 brush.

The lining on this NER 4-4-0 was applied using the compass and pen attachment, starting from the top and moving downwards. I marked points where each line was to be drawn and then drew the straight lines in at the end. Some tidying up with a fine brush was necessary, particular at the lower corners.

This is always a pleasing livery to produce, particularly in 7mm scale. It is perhaps surprising that a railway company could apply this livery to a humble goods engine; although it appears complex it is in fact fairly simple to apply - there is just a lot of it! Care is needed to get the two panels on the tender the same, and to get the wheel lining looking correct.

Chapter Eight

LETTERING AND TRANSFERS

NER 4-wheel saloon built by Dick Tarpey - painted, lined and lettered with my own transfers.

With the model painted and lined, the final job before final varnishing is to add any lettering, numbers, crests or other insignia. This is usually done with transfers. These days, lettering and numbering transfers for many of the old railway companies, as well as the current scene, are available in one form or another. Unfortunately, one of my example liveries, that of the North Staffordshire Railway, was an exception, so a bit of ingenuity was needed in this case. For better-served prototypes, there are four main types of transfer on the market: methylated spirit fixed, pressure fix, waterslide, and rub-down or dry-print.

Methfix

As the name implies, these transfers use a methylated-spirit based adhesive as a fixing agent, and are applied using a 3:1 meths:water mix. I have to say that they are by far and away my favourite type, as they will stick to virtually any surface and are easy and precise to locate. Some modellers don't like them because of the need for the meths/water mix, but this seems a small price to pay for their other virtues.

The transfer has no film, unlike a waterslide type, and the individual characters are printed onto a thin tissue carrier coated with the meths-based gum. This is backed in turn with a heavier paper. In use, each character is cut out with a sharp knife, and the tissue with character is peeled away from the backing paper and placed in position on the model. Once located - you can see what you are doing as the tissue is quite transparent - the whole thing is well-wetted with the meths mixture. The gum sof-

A selection of transfers.

The transfer required is cut around using a sharp knife - lifted from the backing paper, placed in position on the model and soaked in a mixture of meths and water. After a few minutes wash with clean water and remove the backing tissue.

tens almost at once, and the transfer is pressed into place.

If you need to adjust the position slightly, this can be done by re-wetting with the meths mix, and gently 'shunting' the transfer with a fine brush. Once the location is finalised, the transfer is pressed down firmly by rolling with a fingertip, and left to dry. After a few moments, the backing tissue is soaked in water and eased away with tweezers or the tip of a paintbrush. After a couple of hours or so, when the gum under the transfer has hardened, the surface of the model is washed with clean water to remove any excess gum from the paint surface around the characters.

Pressfix

These are similar in many ways to Methfix - they were first introduced by the same firm, PC Models, although others now make similar transfers. Instead of a soluble gum, they are coated with a pressure-sensitive adhesive which is supposed to stick the transfer in place. I say supposed to because, in my experience, this doesn't always happen. These types of trans-

fer have a definite shelf-life, and seem to 'go off ' after a bit. If you are set on using them to letter a model, it pays to use a new sheet - and that means one that your local model shop hasn't had sitting round for ages, either.

To use, these transfers are similar to the Methfix type. The character is cut, peeled and placed as for Methfix, but instead of soaking in meths, the Pressfix type are rubbed down with a ballpoint pen or similar burnishing implement, and the tissue backing soaked and removed. The character should stay behind, firmly stuck to the model. Mostly, it does, but sometimes it will lift and curl; this can occur quite some while after the transfer was (apparently) successfully applied.
These transfers cannot be adjusted for position once they have been rubbed down, which I find to be a major drawback.

As might be apparent from the above, I'm not a great lover of Pressfix transfers. Sometimes, however, I have to use them, as they may be all that is available for certain insignia. Some of the newer types of Pressfix, such as those produced by Woodhead Models,

are much better and seem less prone to dropping off than the PC Models originals, so I would be reasonably happy to use these. Old Pressfix transfers I convert into Methfix types by gently wiping off the pressure adhesive using MEK, then coating with a meths-soluble gum, for which I use Shellac Varnish. This is applied carefully to the required characters, keeping any overlap at the edges to a minimum. The character can then be cut out, applied and adjusted exactly as for a Methfix transfer, which is what it now is.

Waterslide Transfers

Otherwise known as decals, and widely used and accepted by aircraft, road vehicle and military modellers, it is only fairly recently that these have gained acceptance for model railway use by British modellers. In the USA, however, the decal has been the most widely accepted form of transfer for many years, used in conjunction with 'setting solutions' designed to partially dissolve the carrier film, and allowing it to conform closely to surface textures, softening the visible hard edge

Commercial waterslide transfers are widely used by American modellers, and huge ranges are available. The British manufacturers are now starting to catch up, especially for modern prototypes.

of the film. This carrier film, which used to be thick and rather obtrusive, was the main objection to the waterslide transfer. Modern decals, however, have a very much thinner film, and combined with the use of a setting solution such as Carr's 'Transfix', waterslide transfers now give excellent results. Contemporary modellers, particularly, make great use of them, with firms like Fox Transfers providing a huge range in the smaller scales.

Using commercial waterslide transfers is exactly the same as using the home-produced variety described in the lining notes. This means that, for the best adhesion, they need to go onto a smooth, preferably glossy, surface. So you may need to varnish the model before applying these transfers. The transfer design is cut out as close to the outline as possible, to minimise any visible carrier film, soaked in water and slid off the backing paper into place. They are easy to adjust, and once accurately located are pressed down and blotted with a tissue to remove excess water. A little of the setting solution is then brushed on, and the tip of the brush used to snuggle the film down over any surface detail. Don't touch the transfer once the setting solution has been on for more than a couple of minutes, as it becomes sticky for a while, and will always choose to stick to you rather than the model. Once

the transfer is quite dry, it should be varnished over, both to protect the transfer and to bring the finish of the model back to a matt or eggshell from the gloss transfer base coat.

Rub-Down Transfers

Probably best known in the form of commercial 'dryprint' graphics ranges such as Letraset, these are similar to the Pressfix type in that they use a pressure-sensitive adhesive to stick the design in place. However, rather than the double layer tissue/paper backing of Pressfix and similar, dryprints come on a translucent polythene film. In use, the whole sheet is held over the model, the required character being located in the correct place and rubbed down as for the Pressfix. The character should then adhere to the model, allowing the polythene backing to be lifted away. The transferred design is then finally burnished into place by rubbing it through the waxed paper protective sheet supplied with the transfers.

As far as I know, there are very few rub-down transfers currently being produced for locos and coaches, although some wagon markings are made in this form. There used to be quite an extensive range, produced by Kings Cross Models under the trade name 'Kingsprint', and these can sometimes still be found although, so far as I'm aware, they're no longer

being made. Beware of these, as like all rub-down transfers, they have a limited shelf life and most old stock will almost certainly have 'gone off' by now. All these pressure-fix transfers share the major drawback of being non-adjustable; once you've rubbed the character off the backing, then that's it. If you get it wrong, the only answer is to pick off the wrongly-placed transfer using some 'killed' Sellotape, and try again. Don't burnish dryprint down until you're absolutely sure you've got it in the right place.

Although I know of no current range of specialised rub-down transfers for lettering locos and coaches, some of the smaller letterfaces from the commercial graphics ranges can be used as a basis for producing 'one-off' lettering, either direct on the model, or onto transfer film for application as a waterslide. The dryprint characters can be combined with hand-applied pen or brush work for shading, or for adding serifs, crests, etc. The most important thing when making up lettering in this way is to get it in a dead straight line. This is a lot easier to do when using dryprints 'flat' onto decal sheet, which is how the makers intend they should be applied, rather than trying to position them accurately on the model.

Positioning Transfers

Although every step in painting and

COMMERCIALLY AVAILABLE

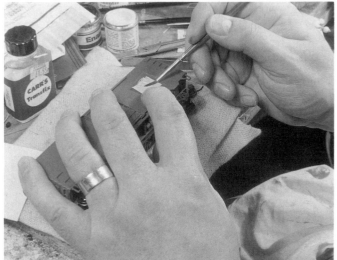

DO IT YOURSELF

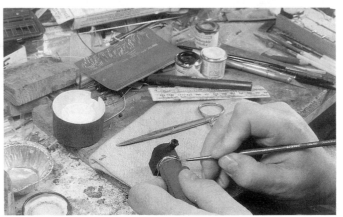

TOP : The transfer design is cut out and placed roughly in position, wetted well and slid onto the model surface. If desired Carrs Transfix will assist with adhesion.

BELOW : Although this sequence shows boiler band lining the application is the same for any area. The required design is drawn onto the painted waterslide transfer paper, cut out, placed in position on the model, wetted well and slid into place removing the backing paper at the same time.

lining a model is important, lettering and numbering can really make or break a paint job. The eye is drawn immediately to anything which is even slightly awry or not quite sitting square, so accurately aligned lettering is vital. Not only do the various characters have to line up both horizontally and vertically, but they must also be correctly spaced.

There are various mechanical ways of getting these things right, but I find that the eye is often the best tool. If you get it *looking right*, then you've won the battle; your eye will tell you when something is only fractionally out, especially if you squint along the line of transfers from an acute angle, rather than looking at them square on.

One technique I use to get letters or, more specifically, numbers, accurately lined up is to use the tissue backing of Methfix transfers as a visual aid. Cut each character out as close as possible to the top, bottom and sides then, if you align the bottom and top edges of the backing, the characters must be in line. Although you can space characters using a rule, I prefer to do this by eye as well, adjusting the positions until it looks correct. Bear in mind that lettering is not always spaced on equal centres, but varies according to the letterform - look at prototype pictures to see how things are arranged. If the number or what-

ever must be centred on a tankside, say, start with the central character or pair of characters, and work outwards. It may be necessary to put a small soft pencil mark on the centreline, together with a faint horizontal pencil line as a guide to getting lettering centred and parallel to the running plate. You can wipe these marks away with a moist tissue once the transfers are in place.

Improvising Transfers

Where there is no suitable transfer lettering available for the paint scheme you are applying, you can sometimes get around the problem by adapting lettering intended for something else. With the large range now available from PC models, I find that there's almost always something to use as a starting point.

As I've already mentioned, there were no suitable transfers for the North Staffordshire 2-4-0T, so this was tackled by modifying some North Eastern Railway lettering, with some hand lettering and a hand-drawn crest. 'North Stafford' is in 5 inch high gold bold capitals in a sans-serif style, shaded vermilion and black. The NER also used a similar block style for lettering tenders, and it soon became apparent that my own 'North Eastern' transfers were very close.
The 'North' was complete in itself, and

'Stafford' used the S, T, R and A from 'Eastern', with the O from another 'North'. That left the two Fs, adapted from the block Es from 'Eastern', and a D, which used a vertical from an N and a hand-drawn cusp. This was applied in gold paint using a fine sable brush, and shaded to match the transfer letters. A little touching-in here and there, and I had some very presentable North Stafford lettering.

Unfortunately, the same dodge couldn't be applied to the distinctive garter crest. The kitmaker suggests basing this on the circular LMS crest, but I found this too large. There was no alternative to doing this by hand, following the black and white picture with colour notes from George Dow's 'North Staffordshire Album'. This is delicate work using fine brushes and perhaps some magnification from a fixed lens or magnifying headband. However, I find it better to work with the naked eye, getting in as close as possible; I'm already on close-up specs for the rest of the time! I made these crests as waterslide transfers as already described for lining, using the same Madder Lake-sprayed decal film that I had prepared for making the boiler bands. After allowing 24 hours for the paint to dry thoroughly, these transfers were cut out accurately around their outline, and applied to the model as already described.

Unlike some companies, the Midland liked to get the MR exactly in the middle of the panels.

VARNISHING AND WEATHERING

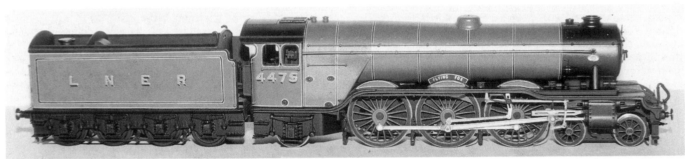

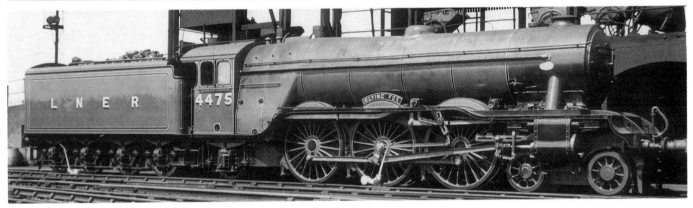

Top : Scatchbuilt 7mm LNER (ex.GNR) D2. Although not shown, I built this in several sub-assemblies to make life easier. Painted in Floquil Engine Black, it is varnished with Floquil Flat Finish showing the lovely sheen which is possible using this product. Middle : See the bits on page 10. Eggshell finish, obtained by mixing satin with a little matt. I was lucky to find this prototype picture to ensure accuracy.

Varnishes were applied to prototype locos and stock to protect the underlying paint, as well as to produce a deep and lustrous finish. In liveries such as Crimson Lake, the varnish brings the colour to life, giving it the full richness for which the livery was famous. The same effect will be produced on a correctly-varnished model, so it is well worth experimenting with the various varnishes available.

Properly applied, the varnish really finishes off the model, protecting and enhancing the livery underneath. It will bring together the various elements - sprayed or brushed paint, pen-ruled lining and transfers - into one finish that makes the paint job look 'all of a piece'. However, it's no good just applying any old varnish any old how. For a start, some thought must

be given to the appropriate degree of finish for each individual model. High gloss would look pretty silly on a humble coal wagon, for instance. There are a lot of factors to take into account when deciding the right sort of finish. Pre-grouping engines for instance, in the age when plentiful cheap labour was available, were kept in a state of cleanliness that has declined ever since. Hence, for the NSR 2-4-0T, modelled as running in 1903, and the MR 0-6-0 of about the same date, a relatively 'high' finish was applied, with gloss and satin varnish mixed in a 1:2 ratio as described below.

All of the main paint manufacturers produce varnishes to complement their paint ranges, although some are more suited as finishing coats than others. I rarely use a full gloss varnish

for this job, as to my eyes it generally looks wholly wrong in the smaller scales. For 4mm, I aim for an eggshell or satin finish, shiny enough to give a bit of sheen but a long way from a high gloss. For 7mm, I find that the larger surface areas will allow a slightly glossier finish without ending up with too many reflections. Coaches, particularly flush-sided ones, also have large areas of relatively flat surface that seem able to take a glossier finish, even in 4mm. The naturally reflective nature of the glazing makes coaches appear rather 'brighter' anyway, and a slightly higher gloss adds to this effect.

I have arrived at my varnish finishes by experiment, and find that by selecting and mixing varnishes, I can obtain just about any degree of finish

Don't be put off from experimenting with varnishes not necessarily associated with the hobby. Recently I have found that the Ronseal varnishes are particularly good.

from dead matt to a full gloss. Had they still been available, I would have recommended the Floquil range of varnishes without hesitation, as they were every bit as good as the paints. However, unless you are holidaying in the USA and can smuggle a few jars back with you, we are stuck with those varnishes offered by British makers.

Most of the paintmakers offer gloss, satin and matt within their ranges, and these can usually be mixed to get intermediate finishes. The exception is Humbrol, where the gloss varnish is a polyurethane type and the matt is enamel-based, and these two won't mix. Humbrol satin is, fortunately, about right, and if needed can be made a little glossier by removing some of the matting agent from the bottom of an undisturbed tin before mixing. Humbrol apart, the other makes can be freely mixed within their own ranges. I usually use matt and gloss, adjusting the proportions to give the degree of finish required. When trying out varnish mixes, don't forget to note the proportions of each mix so that when you hit the right one you can repeat it as required.

It is also worth looking around at what non-specific varnishes are available. After learning from several modellers that they got good results from 'Ronseal' polyurethane varnish, obtainable from DIY shops and intended to protect wood, I decided to give it a go. The MR 0-6-0 demonstration loco was finished with it, with perfectly satisfactory results. It needs thinning with a good quality thinner for airbrush use - I used Cherry Paints thinner in a 50/50 dilution. I have also mixed Ronseals gloss and satin finishes, as described above, to get the desired degree of finish.

Spraying Varnishes

I apply varnish through the airbrush much as for paints. Where necessary, it is thinned in exactly the same way as paint, using the thinner appropriate to the range of varnish being used. Effectively, these varnishes *are* paints, with the colour simply left out. When spraying varnish through the airbrush, it is possible to vary the finish simply by regulating the air pressure and spraying distance. Spraying with high pressure from twelve to fifteen inches away gives a dull finish, as the finely divided varnish dries on contact to give a relatively matt surface. Spraying with lower pressure, close in, gives bigger droplets that stay wet long enough to flow out, giving a smoother and glossier finish.

Spray cans of varnish are also available, but as varnish ideally needs to be applied with a softer spray than is given by an aerosol, these are not always a good idea. The trouble is that, using an aerosol, the varnish will come out too fast, thus tending to build up around the various bits and pieces which stick out of our models, while failing to penetrate some corners. The softer spray of the airbrush gives a better, more even finish to the whole model and it is possible to vary the varnish on different parts, either by adjusting distance and pressure, or by masking-up as for painting and using different varnish mixes on different parts of the model - matt on the smokebox and cab roof, and gloss on a boiler, for instance.

Weathering

Until fairly recently I had not been too convinced over the value of weathering models, preferring to see them

Tom Harland is to blame for this! Nicely done though, and when running on Bramblewick it really blends in with the atmosphere created.

in all their glory. After all, when you've put a great deal of hard work into getting the paintwork and lining looking just right, covering them with a layer of grot seems a bit like masochism. However, when weathering is applied properly, it does give the model a quality of realism that can enhance not just the individual loco or coach, but the whole model railway, especially if all the elements are weathered in the same way.

One has only to look at a layout like 'Bramblewick', where Tom Harland treats every part of it to a subtle process of weathering and toning-in, making the whole thing look not just wonderfully realistic, but also as if all the bits really belong together. The only snag, and it's quite a big one for us lesser mortals, is that Tom is a professional artist, and has the 'eye' to

recreate on the model the subtle shades and colours of the real thing. I have to admit that when Tom first started to weather some of the locomotives that I had built and painted for the layout, I was just a tiny bit bothered, having put a lot of time into finishing them. Now I'm convinced that a good weathering job is worth the effort, especially for locos or stock intended to run on a layout rather than sit in a showcase. That's not to say that there's no place for the showcase model; I still like the odd 'unblemished' loco, and I keep one or two of mine in this state.

Weathering Techniques

I generally rely on two main weathering techniques, dry brushing and very soft overspraying. Both methods

give a very subtle effect, with the 'dirt' building up in corners, around strapping, rivets, pipework and so on. Areas which, on the prototype, are hard to clean. This gives the look of an item of stock which has got dirty and then been cleaned. Clean, but not clean, if you see what I mean.

The drybrush technique uses slightly thinned paint - the brush is loaded, then most of the paint is wiped off on a tissue. The result is that paint will only be dragged off the brush when it meets raised surface detail, rather than leaving an overall layer of paint. The more paint there is on the brush, the more will be left behind on the model. Drybrushing should only be applied lightly, and can be used over most of the paintwork. Drybrush technique can be used to 'highlight' an overall coat of weathering applied by airbrush - as below. Normal wet brush techniques are also occasionally used for jobs like picking out individual fittings or for adding rust patches and oil or lime stains.

My favourite basic weathering technique, however, is to use a thin mix of matt paint sprayed on at very low pressure through the airbrush. It is possible, under these conditions, to get in very close to the model and get the paint into those nooks and crannies where the dirt would accumulate on the prototype. I find that this gives a very subtle result, ranging from the slightest dulling of the livery to a real coat of filth, as required.

There is another technique gaining increased acceptance, which is to use powders to apply colour. These can either be purpose-made weathering powders, or ground-up pastels or chalks. The snag is that they don't stick to anything remotely resembling a glossy surface. They are applied with a soft brush and held in place with a light coat of varnish. The varnish needs to be dead matt and sprayed on at ultra-low pressure, if you don't want to blow all the powder off again!

Weathering Materials

I generally use the same types of paint for weathering models as I do for the main paint job. In choosing appropriate colours, I find that darker browns are about right in most instances, but they need varying. It is important to choose the right shade for the right job. I have found that Humbrol 'track colour' is a good general purpose shade, that can be tinted or overlaid to get the required effects. By keeping the spraying mix very thin, it is possible to spray on successive colours to build up an effect without disturbing the overall look of the model too much. Using well thinned matt paint as advocated means that the weathering will dry very quickly, virtually within seconds. It may be worth considering a water-based paint such as gouache for weathering, as if you don't like the effect you arrive at, you

Looking very miserable.

D16 at Stratford works.

can simply wash it off and start again.

Weathering powders are available from Carr's in a variety of shades of mud, rust, dust, coal dust, etc. These can be mixed together to give any desired colour. They are actually very finely ground paint pigments and some are quite potent, a little going a long way. You can also make weathering powders by rubbing artists pastels on a piece of coarse sandpaper or a small file. Pastels come in a huge range of shades and can be bought individually from art shops.

Applying Weathering

The best strategy when applying weathering is not to put too much on at once, but rather to aim to build up the effect gently. Keep standing back and looking at the model to check the overall effect. The only colour I *never* use is black. Take a look around you and you will not find any natural black. Most 'blacks' are actually shades of blue, grey or brown. Otherwise, I just keep adding colour in very small amounts, always working towards a specific idea of the look I'm after, and often working to a prototype photo.

When considering how much and what sort of weathering to apply, it's important to think about how the prototype got into the weathered state. Before it weathered in service, a real loco or coach would have started in pristine condition 'ex-works'. This is why it is best to start with the model

in 'good condition', rather trying to actually *paint* something as run down, which I for one find very difficult. To get the look of an in service' item of stock, which has become dirty and been cleaned, repeatedly, it is necessary to consider how this process has been carried out. Has the loco or whatever always been kept clean, or allowed to get grubby then been spruced up? How was it cleaned? What geographical area is it running in, and is the track ballasted with a 'clean' material like stone, or a 'dirty' one like ash? These factors make a difference to the amount and colour of the dust and dirt thrown up underneath. And there is always the loco or item of stock that has been neglected, with rust patches, lime streaks, and caked-on oil and grease as well as the inevitable dirt.

If you want to arrive at a convincing finish, a lot of thought and experiment will be required to give the right formula. Perhaps this is a final role for your 'test piece' plastic loco body, which can be used to try out different weathering techniques and colours until you hit on the right combination. If you're not sure, err on the side of subtlety and avoid brashness. Often, toning down the paintwork is really all that is needed. Perhaps the most difficult thing is knowing when to stop, so it is important to take time and assess how it looks after each pass of the airbrush. As always, let the eye be the judge. When it looks right, it's time to stop.

Don't be tempted to keep on trying for that little bit more, as it will almost certainly be a little bit too much.

In Conclusion....

From talking to fellow-modellers and demonstrating at exhibitions, it is clear that the painting and lining of locos and coaches causes a lot of us considerable anguish and heartache. While this book describes only one approach to the job - mine - and thus may not answer some questions on the subject, it will hopefully suggest a range of tried and tested answers to many of the problems associated with the finishing of small scale models. The most valuable asset for the aspiring loco-painter is confidence in his own ability, and the only way to gain that confidence is to practice. The important thing is to have a go and try your hand. If all else fails and you make a real pig's ear of it, there's always the paintstripper.

That said, you'll be surprised how rarely it comes to that. Most times you'll be able to rescue the job, and even complete disasters count as part of the learning curve. We railway modellers need to wear so many hats and develop so many skills that it's sometimes a wonder we ever finish anything. The trouble with painting and lining is that it's such a *visible* skill. Your electrics, for instance, might be a real mess, but they're hidden below the baseboard and so long as they work, nobody notices. Get a line wonky on a cabside, though, and everyone and his brother will take great delight in pointing it out.

If I had to emphasise one thing, it would be the importance of approaching the job in as relaxed a manner as possible. This can be difficult when things aren't going well, but it is perhaps best to put it to one side and do something else. I often find that just leaving a job that is giving me problems until the next day can make all the difference.

Part of being relaxed is not being impatient. There is no point in trying to rush through a painting and lining job, as whatever you do, there will have to be lengthy delays while the paint dries. For example, the LMS coach in BR crimson and cream took me about five working hours to paint, from cleaning process to final coat of varnish. But it actually took five *days*, to allow proper drying times. Unless the need is urgent, it never pays to rush.

As with many of the finer things in life, the skill of painting and lining is not something which can be acquired overnight. I've been painting my own models now getting on for twenty years, and I'm still learning and experimenting. If the reader of this book has learnt something from these pages, and I sincerely hope he will, then the effort of writing will have been worthwhile. Happy Modelling!

Weathering comes in a variety of forms.

EXAMPLES

Top : Alan Gibson M Class in simple Somerset and Dorset livery. Middle : LSWR T9 in Urie livery. Bottom : Another loco built as a challenge, both this Gresley LNER P1 Class, and the V2 illustrated earlier, where built when I had time to endulge myself.

Top : A D&S 6-wheel NER luggage brake. It's very satisfying to paint and line out a model and then add your own transfers. Bottom : The first loco I ever built, but now much modified

SUPPLIERS INDEX

AIRBRUSHES

Badger airbrushes and accessories:-

Richard Khonstam Ltd.
13-15A High Street
Hemel Hempstead
Herts
HP1 3AD   Tel 0442 - 61721

Paasche airbrushes and accessories

Rotring UK
The Airbrush and Spray Centre Ltd.
39 Littlehampton Road
Worthing
Sussex
BN13 1JQ   Tel 0903 - 266991

PAINTS

Cherry Paints
Micrologica Systems Ltd.
Ronty Brig
Glenquiech
By Forfar
DD8 3UA   Tel 0575 - 4424

RailMatch Paints
Howes of Oxford
9-10 Broad Street
Oxford
OX1 3AJ   Tel 0865 - 242407

Limited supplies of
Floquil
Dave Smith
Midland Railway Centre
339 Bath Road
Kettering
Northants NN16 9LJ
Tel: 0536 410536

Accu Flex paints -
See Badger details above.

TRANSFERS

P.C. Models
2 Marsh Lane
Birmingham   Tel 021-373-3215

Fox Transfers
Old School House
12 Brougham Street
Leicester
LE1 2BA Tel 0533 - 626868

PLAIN WATERSLIDE
TRANSFER PAPER

H.G.Hannant Ltd.
Trafalgar House
29-31 Trafalgar Street
Lowestoft
Suffolk
NR32 3AT Tel 0502 - 565688/
517444 - Ask for TF-0 Clear Trim
Film

Impetus
PO Box 1472
Coggeshall
Colchester
CO6 1UQ

Cellux Masking Tape:-
from the author at
'Dinsdale'
3 Caverstede Road
Walton
Peterborough
PE4 6EX

Ecobra Lining Pens:-
from the author as above.